THE   BOOK   OF

LIGHT
DESSERTS

THE   BOOK   OF

LIGHT DESSERTS

ANNE SHEASBY

Photographed by
JON STEWART

a Salamander book
Published by Salamander Books Limited
LONDON

Published 1994 by Salamander Books Limited
129-137 York Way, London N7 9LG, United Kingdom

© Salamander Books Ltd 1994

ISBN 0-86101-757-9

Distributed by Hodder & Stoughton Services, PO Box 6,
Mill Road, Dunton Green, Sevenoaks, Kent TN13 2XX

Managing Editor: Felicity Jackson
Art Director: Roger Daniels
Editor: Barbara Croxford
Photographer: Jon Stewart, assisted by Nicole Mai
Home Economists: Kerenza Harries and Jo Craig
Typeset by: BMD Graphics, Hemel Hempstead
Colour separation by: Scantrans Pte. Ltd, Singapore
Printed in Belgium by Proost International Book Production

ACNOWLEDGEMENTS

The publishers would like to thank the following for their help:
Barbara Stewart at Prop Exchange, Unit F,
51 Calthorpe Street, London WC1

Notes:
All spoon measurements are equal.
1 teaspoon = 5 ml spoon
1 tablespoon = 15 ml spoon.

CONTENTS

COMPANION VOLUMES OF INTEREST:

INTRODUCTION

A cookery book on the subject of light desserts probably seems like a contradiction in terms. How can a dessert be light and low in calories and fat, yet still be appealing and delectable to taste?

Nowadays, with the enormous range of fresh fruits and natural foods readily available, it is easy to create healthy desserts which are light and attractive, too.

The mouthwatering desserts in this book will appeal to everyone. Most of the recipes are economical as well as being quick and easy to make. Special occasion desserts require slightly more costly ingredients and take longer to prepare, but they are well worth the extra effort.

Recipes include classic desserts, childrens favourites, everyday delights and unusual exotic desserts, each one beautifully illustrated in full colour and with step-by-step instructions.

Enjoy all these tempting desserts, whilst cutting down on your calorie and fat intakes, and you won't even notice the difference.

INGREDIENTS – LIGHT DESSERTS

Nowadays, healthy eating plays a vital role in our general well being and adopting good eating habits is important.

The word 'dessert' conjures up a glorious picture of a delightful finale to complement any enjoyable meal. Light desserts can be just as tempting and delicious by making a few simple changes to the ingredients.

All the low fat and low calorie ingredients used in the recipes are readily available, so you won't have to venture any further than your local supermarket.

MILK

Milk is a nutritious food and provides a good source of protein, as well as many vitamins and minerals. It is an essential ingredient in some of the recipes but instead of full-fat milk, skimmed milk or semi-skimmed milk has been used.

Skimmed milk contains a fat content of no more than 0.3 per cent and all the nutrients of whole milk with the exception of the fat-soluble vitamins.

Semi-skimmed milk contains 1.5–1.8% milk fat.

Evaporated milk is canned milk which has had a large percentage of its water content removed. It contains no added sugar and is a rich source of vitamin D.

Reduced fat or 'light' evaporated milk is used in some of the recipes. It contains less than half the fat content of ordinary evaporated milk.

YOGURT

Yogurt is a delicious food which is often served on its own or as an accompaniment to fresh fruit.

Natural yogurt has a slightly acidic but refreshing flavour that is excellent in desserts. Very low fat natural yogurt contains less than 0.5% fat and low fat natural yogurt contains 0.5–2% fat.

Greek yogurt, which has a higher fat content of 9–10%, is used in some of the recipes and is ideal as a substitute for cream.

REDUCED FAT CREAMS

Cream is an ingredient commonly associated with desserts. In this book reduced fat creams, which taste as good as ordinary creams but contain fewer calories and half the fat, have been used.

FROMAGE FRAIS

Fromage frais is a fresh white curd cheese made from pasteurized skimmed cow's milk. It has a very soft consistency and makes an excellent base for many desserts or is an ideal substitute for cream. There are several types of fromage frais available and the two most common types have been used in these recipes.

Very low fat fromage frais contains approximately 1% fat and has a mildly acidic flavour.

Low fat fromage frais contains approximately 8% fat and has a more creamy flavour (due to the addition of cream when it is produced).

SOFT CHEESE

The recipes have used two types of soft cheese.

Skimmed milk soft cheese is very low fat soft cheese which has a very low fat content and therefore a less creamy flavour than full fat or cream cheese.

Low fat soft cheese is a soft cheese with a low fat content and a slightly more creamy flavour.

Cottage cheese has been used in some of the recipes because it is an excellent low fat ingredient for some desserts.

LOW FAT SPREAD

Some fat is essential in our diet, but saturated fats such as butter, hard margarine, lard and suet should be avoided. Polyunsaturated margarines are a better choice but we should be cutting down on these, too.

In place of butter or margarine which contain very high fat contents, low fat spread has been used as an alternative. It generally contains half the fat of butter or margarine and is suitable for baking, melting and pastry-making.

Very low fat spread is not suitable for baking or pastry-making.

EGGS

Eggs are an excellent source of protein. However, egg yolks contain a high percentage of fat so be careful not to eat too many.

SUGAR AND HONEY

Sugar is high in calories but contains few nutrients, so we should cut down on it in our diet as much as possible.

Three types of sugar have been used

in the recipes – caster sugar, soft brown sugar and icing sugar, each having their own characteristic flavour.

In some recipes honey has been used in place of sugar. Honey is naturally sweeter than sugar, so less tends to be used in recipes. It also has a pleasant taste of its own.

FLOUR
In some of the recipes, 100% whole-meal flour has been used. It contains more dietary fibre than white flour and has a delicious flavour, too.

FRUIT
Fruit is a ready source of energy, and most of it is low in calories, too. Vitamins and minerals are present in most fruits, as well as natural fruit sugar or fructose.

Fresh, canned or dried fruit can be put to numerous uses in light desserts.

The natural sugar and acids found in fruit contribute to the flavour and texture of the dessert and many fruits are a good source of fibre, particularly if their edible skins are left on.

Choose fresh, plump, firm fruits avoiding wrinkled, mouldy or bruised fruits as these will spoil the flavour of the dessert. Many fruits are available all year round nowadays, but canned and frozen fruits make excellent substitutes when fresh fruits are unavailable. Always remember to wash and dry the fruit before using.

Dried fruit is sweeter and richer than fresh fruit so only small amounts are needed for light desserts.

NUTS
Nuts are a good source of energy, high in protein, carbohydrates and fat, which means they are high in calories, too! Nuts have been used in some of the recipes but the quantities have been kept low.

CAROB
Use carob in place of chocolate or cocoa to reduce the fat content in desserts. Carob, produced from the carob bean, is available in bar form or as flour. It is naturally sweeter than chocolate and free from caffeine.

LOW FAT CUSTARD
Low fat custard powder or ready made custard is readily available and is an ideal alternative to the full fat variety.

SUGAR-FREE JELLIES
Sugar-free jelly crystals reduce the sugar and calorie content of a dessert.

> The serving suggestions at the end of most recipes are **not** included in the calorie counts and fat figures.

──── RASPBERRY BAVAROIS ────

400 g (14 oz) can raspberries in fruit juice
135 g (4½ oz) raspberry jelly tablet
425 ml (15 fl oz/1¾ cups) reduced fat evaporated milk
fresh raspberries and mint sprigs, to decorate

Drain raspberries over a bowl, reserving fruit juice. In a measuring jug, make juice up to 300 ml (10 fl oz/1¼ cups) with water.

Put juice and jelly tablet in a saucepan and place on a low heat. When jelly has dissolved, remove from heat and leave to cool. In a large bowl, whisk evaporated milk until thick. Add raspberries and jelly and mix well.

Pour mixture into a serving bowl. Chill in the refrigerator until set. Decorate with raspberries and mint sprigs before serving.

Serves 6.

Total Cals/Kj: 914/3873   Total fat: 18.2 g
Cals/Kj per portion: 152/646   Fat per portion: 3.0 g

MUESLI CHEESECAKE

45 g (1½ oz/9 teaspoons) low fat spread, melted
115 g (4 oz/1¼ cups) sugar-free muesli
3 teaspoons powdered gelatine
350 g (12 oz/1½ cups) skimmed milk soft cheese
55 g (2 oz/¼ cup) caster sugar
grated rind and juice of 1 lemon
150 ml (5 fl oz/⅔ cup) reduced fat double
    (heavy) cream
fresh fruit, such as redcurrants, strawberries,
    figs and peaches, to decorate

In a bowl, mix melted low fat spread with muesli. Press mixture over base of a 20 cm (8 in) loose-bottomed tin and chill in the refrigerator.

Sprinkle gelatine over 3 tablespoons water in a small bowl and leave for 2-3 minutes to soften. Stand bowl in a saucepan of hot water and stir until gelatine has dissolved. Cool slightly. In a bowl, beat soft cheese, sugar, lemon rind and juice together, then stir in gelatine. In a separate bowl, whip cream lightly and fold into cheese mixture.

Pour it over muesli base, levelling surface. Return to the refrigerator to set. To serve, remove cheesecake from tin, place on a serving plate and decorate with fresh fruit.

Serves 6.

Total Cals/Kj: 1467/6246   Total fat: 63.5 g
Cals/Kj per portion: 245/1041   Fat per portion: 10.5 g

MOCHA POTS

3 teaspoons cornflour
150 ml (5 fl oz/²⁄₃ cup) skimmed milk
55 g (2 oz/¹⁄₄ cup) caster sugar
85 g (3 oz) plain (dark) chocolate, broken into pieces
½ teaspoon instant coffee granules
300 ml (10 fl oz/1¹⁄₄ cups) very low fat fromage frais
kumquat slices and chocolate vermicelli, to decorate

In a saucepan, blend cornflour with milk. Add sugar and chocolate and heat gently, stirring continuously, until mixture thickens. Cook for a further 3 minutes. Set aside to cool slightly.

Dissolve coffee in 1 tablespoon warm water. When chocolate mixture is cool, add coffee and fromage frais. Stir until thoroughly combined.

Spoon mixture into individual glass serving dishes and chill in the refrigerator before serving. When ready to serve, decorate each dessert with kumquat slices and chocolate vermicelli.

Serves 4.

Total Cals/Kj: 923/3974   Total fat: 25.6 g
Cals/Kj per portion: 231/994   Fat per portion: 6.4 g

Note: If kumquats are not available, orange slices can be used as decoration.

—BAKED APPLES WITH PRUNES—

4 large cooking apples
175 g (6 oz/1 cup) dried prunes, finely chopped
4 teaspoons clear honey
2 teaspoons ground mixed spice

Preheat oven to 180C (350F/Gas 4). Wash
and dry apples, but do not peel. Remove core
using an apple corer, then make a shallow cut
through the skin around each apple.

Stand apples in an ovenproof dish. Fill apple
cavities with prunes, pushing them down
firmly. Top with honey and sprinkle each
apple with mixed spice.

Put 4 tablespoons water around apples and
bake in oven for 45-60 minutes until soft.
Serve immediately with low fat yogurt,
custard or reduced fat cream sprinkled with
cinnamon.

Serves 4.

Total Cals/Kj: 538/2279   Total fat: 1.9 g
Cals/Kj per portion: 135/569   Fat per portion: 0.4 g

Variation: Dried figs may be used in place of
prunes, if wished.

RED FRUIT MEDLEY

115 g (4 oz/½ cup) caster sugar
225 g (8 oz) strawberries
225 g (8 oz) cherries
8 red dessert plums
2 red-skinned eating apples
225 g (8 oz) raspberries
fresh mint, to decorate

Put 425 ml (15 fl oz/1¾ cups) water into a saucepan with the sugar. Dissolve sugar over a low heat, stirring occasionally. Bring mixture to the boil and boil rapidly, uncovered, for 10 minutes. Set aside to cool.

To prepare fruit, cut strawberries in half and stone cherries. Halve and stone plums. Core apples and cut into chunks. Place all the fruit in a large serving dish.

Pour cooled sugar mixture over fruit and stir gently to mix. Chill in the refrigerator before serving. To serve, decorate with mint and serve chilled with Greek yogurt.

Serves 6.

Total Cals/Kj: 923/3890   Total fat: 1.6 g
Cals/Kj per portion: 154/648   Fat per portion: 0.2 g

—————— LIME CHEESE JELLY ——————

135 g (4½ oz) lime jelly tablet
225 g (8 oz/1 cup) low fat soft cheese
grated rind and juice of 1 lime
lemon and lime slices, to decorate

In a saucepan, dissolve jelly tablet in 300 ml
(10 fl oz/1¼ cups) boiling water, then make
up liquid to 550 ml (20 fl oz/2½ cups) with
water. Allow to cool.

In a blender or food processor, blend cooled
jelly, cheese and grated lime rind and juice
together. Pour into a wetted 850 ml (30 fl oz/
3¾ cup) mould. Refrigerate until set.

When ready to serve, turn jelly out onto a
serving dish and decorate with lemon and
lime slices.

Serves 4.

Total Cals/Kj: 654/2758   Total fat: 15.3 g
Cals/Kj per portion: 164/689   Fat per portion: 3.8 g

Variation: Try using a lemon jelly tablet and
lemon rind and juice for a slightly different
flavour.

—CHERRY YOGURT SYLLABUB—

400 g (14 oz) can cherries
450 ml (14 fl oz/2 cups) low fat cherry yogurt
150 ml (5 fl oz/²⁄₃ cup) dry white wine
150 ml (5 fl oz/²⁄₃ cup) reduced fat double
  (heavy) cream

Drain and stone the cherries.

In a blender or food processor, blend yogurt, wine and cherries together. In a large bowl, whip cream until thick. Gradually fold into the fruit mixture.

Spoon cherry and yogurt mixture into 6 individual glasses. Chill in the refrigerator for at least 2 hours before serving. Serve with sponge fingers.

Serves 6.

Total Cals/Kj: 1158/4881   Total fat: 39.1 g
Cals/Kj per portion: 193/814   Fat per portion: 6.5 g

Variation: Reserve a few of the cherries for decoration, if wished.

LEMON FRUIT KEBABS

1 small pineapple
3 kiwi fruit
½ small melon
2 peaches
12 large strawberries
grated rind and juice of 1 lemon
3 teaspoons cornflour
6 teaspoons caster sugar
lime slices, to decorate (optional)

To prepare fruit, cut pineapple into thick slices, then peel and discard core and cut flesh into chunks.

Peel kiwi fruit and cut into quarters. Peel and remove seeds from melon and cut flesh into chunks. Peel and stone peaches and cut into chunks. Halve strawberries. Thread fruit onto 12 kebab sticks, place on a serving dish, cover and refrigerate. To make sauce, in a measuring jug make lemon juice up to 300 ml (10 fl oz/1¼ cups) with water.

In a saucepan, blend cornflour and sugar with lemon juice and water. Add grated lemon rind. Bring to the boil over a low heat, stirring continuously until the mixture thickens. Cook for a further 3 minutes. Serve hot lemon sauce immediately with fruit kebabs. Serve 2 kebabs per person and decorate with lime slices, if wished.

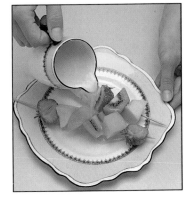

Serves 6.

Total Cals/Kj: 660/2851
Cals/Kj per portion: 110/475

Total fat: 2.5 g
Fat per portion: 0.4 g

-GRAPEFRUIT YOGURT SUNDAE-

85 g (3 oz) semi-sweet wheatmeal biscuits
55 g (2 oz/¼ cup) low fat spread, melted
85 g (3 oz/3 cups) bran flakes
400 g (14 oz) can grapefruit in fruit juice, drained and
    finely chopped
300 ml (10 fl oz/1 ¼ cups) low fat plain yogurt
grapefruit segments and mint sprigs, to decorate

Crush biscuits to crumbs, then mix with
melted low fat spread and bran flakes.

In a bowl, mix together grapefruit and yogurt.
Layer yogurt mixture and crunch mixture in
6 glass dishes, finishing with a crunch layer.

Chill in the refrigerator until ready to serve.
Decorate desserts with grapefruit segments
and mint sprigs.

Serves 6.

Total Cals/Kj: 1201/5037   Total fat: 43.8 g
Cals/Kj per portion: 200/839   Fat per portion: 7.3 g

Variation: Try using other types of crunchy
cereal in place of bran flakes.

TANGERINE FLUFF

12.5 g (½ oz) packet sugar-free tangerine jelly crystals
200 ml (7 fl oz/¾ cup) reduced fat evaporated milk
225 g (8 oz/1 cup) low fat soft cheese
tangerine segments and mint sprigs, to decorate

Dissolve jelly crystals in 300 ml (10 fl oz/
1¼ cups) boiling water, then make liquid up
to 425 ml (15 fl oz/1¾ cups) with cold water.
Leave aside until just beginning to set.

In a bowl, whip evaporated milk until thick,
then gradually beat it into soft cheese until
thoroughly combined. Fold jelly into the
cheese mixture until evenly mixed.

Pour into a wetted 850 ml (30 fl oz/3¾ cup)
mould. Chill in the refrigerator until set.
When ready to serve, turn out of the mould
onto a serving dish and decorate with
tangerine segments and mint sprigs.

Serves 4.

Total Cals/Kj: 568/2170   Total fat: 23.3 g
Cals/Kj per portion: 142/543   Fat per portion: 5.8 g

PEACH TRIFLE

6 teaspoons reduced sugar strawberry jam
5 trifle sponge cakes
400 g (14 oz) can peach slices in fruit juice
6 teaspoons sweet sherry
12.5 g (½ oz) packet sugar-free strawberry
   jelly crystals
3 teaspoons cornflour
3 teaspoons sugar
pinch of salt
3 egg yolks
450 ml (16 fl oz/2 cups) skimmed milk
150 ml (5 fl oz/⅔ cup) reduced fat double
   (heavy) cream, lightly whipped
fresh fruit, to decorate

Spread jam on cakes; cut into fingers.

Place fingers in base of a glass serving dish.
Drain peaches, reserving juice. Mix together
peach juice and sherry and pour over sponge
cakes. Arrange peach slices on top. Dissolve
jelly crystals in 300 ml (10 fl oz/1¼ cups)
boiling water, then make up to 550 ml
(20 fl oz/2½ cups) with cold water. Cool and
then pour jelly over sponge cakes. Chill in
the refrigerator until set. Meanwhile, blend
cornflour, sugar, salt and egg yolks with 3
tablespoons of the milk. In a saucepan, heat
remaining milk, bring to the boil, then pour
onto blended mixture, stirring well.

Return mixture to pan and bring to the boil,
stirring, until thick. Boil for 1 minute. Pour
into a basin to cool, cover with a damp
cloth. When cool, spread it over the jelly.
Top with cream; decorate with fruit.

Serves 6.

Total Cals/Kj: 1479/6006   Total fat: 62.2 g
Cals/Kj per portion: 246/1001   Fat per portion: 10.3 g

Variation: Sprinkle chopped nuts over the
top, but remember this will add calories.

-CHOC ORANGE BLANCMANGE-

12 teaspoons cornflour
9 teaspoons caster sugar
550 ml (20 fl oz/2½ cups) skimmed milk
115 g (4 oz) plain (dark) chocolate drops
grated rind of 1 large orange
orange slices and rind, to decorate

Blend cornflour and sugar with 2 tablespoons of the milk. In a saucepan, heat remaining milk and chocolate drops together until boiling.

Pour onto cornflour mixture, stirring well. Return mixture to saucepan and bring to the boil, stirring continuously until mixture thickens. Cook for a further 3 minutes. Add orange rind and stir well. Pour into a wetted 685 ml (24 fl oz/3 cup) mould and leave to set. Chill in the refrigerator until ready to serve.

When ready to serve, turn out of mould onto a serving dish and decorate with orange slices and rind.

Serves 6.

Total Cals/Kj: 1159/4956   Total fat: 34.5 g
Cals/Kj per portion: 193/826   Fat per portion: 5.7 g

Note: To unmould the dessert, immerse the mould in hot water for 2-3 seconds and place a wetted serving plate on top of mould. Hold in position and quickly invert together.

FIVE-FRUIT SALAD

½ melon
2 red-skinned eating apples
12 fresh dates
175 g (6 oz) green seedless grapes
400 g (14 oz) can apricot halves in fruit juice
425 ml (15 fl oz/1¾ cups) tropical fruit juice

To prepare fruit, peel and remove seeds from melon and cut flesh into chunks. Core apples and cut into chunks.

Halve and stone dates. Halve grapes, if they are large in size. Drain apricots, reserving juice. Place all the fruit in a large glass serving dish.

Mix reserved apricot juice with tropical fruit juice, pour over fruit and stir gently to mix. Cover and leave to stand in a cool place for 2-3 hours before serving. Serve with low fat fromage frais.

Serves 6.

Total Cals/Kj: 815/3490   Total fat: 1.9 g
Cals/Kj per portion: 136/582   Fat per portion: 0.3 g

APPLE & GINGER CRISP

450 g (1 lb) cooking apples
25 g (1 oz/2 tablespoons) soft brown sugar
55 g (2 oz/¼ cup) low fat spread
6 teaspoons clear honey
175 g (6 oz/2 cups) rolled oats
2 teaspoons ground ginger

Preheat oven to 180C (350F/Gas 4). Peel, core and slice apples. Place in a saucepan with 2 tablespoons water. Cook gently until apples have softened.

Add sugar and mix well. Spoon stewed apples into a 1.2 litre (40 fl oz/5 cup) ovenproof dish and set aside. In a saucepan, melt low fat spread and honey together. Add oats and ginger and stir until thoroughly combined.

Place oat mixture on top of apples. Bake in oven for 30 minutes until golden brown and crispy on top. Serve hot or cold with low fat custard or reduced fat cream.

Serves 6.

Total Cals/Kj: 1202/5020   Total Fat: 35.8 g
Cals/Kj per portion: 200/836   Fat per portion: 5.9 g

——PLUM & APPLE MOUSSE——

350 g (12 oz) cooking apples
350 g (12 oz) plums
2 tablespoons lemon juice
3 teaspoons powdered gelatine
12 teaspoons clear honey
300 ml (10 fl oz/1¼ cups) low fat plain yogurt
apple slices and mint sprigs, to decorate

Peel, core and slice apples. Halve and stone plums. Place in a saucepan with lemon juice and 2 tablespoons water. Cover and heat gently over a low heat until soft.

Cool slightly, then purée in a blender or food processor. Cool completely. Sprinkle gelatine over 3 tablespoons water in a small bowl and leave for 2-3 minutes to soften. Stand bowl in a saucepan of hot water and stir until gelatine has dissolved. Cool slightly.

Stir dissolved gelatine into plum and apple mixture, with the honey and yogurt and mix well. Spoon mixture into individual glass serving dishes and chill in the refrigerator until set. Decorate with apple slices and mint sprigs and serve with sponge fingers, if wished.

Serves 4.

Total Cals/Kj: 605/2560   Total fat: 3.0 g
Cals/Kj per portion: 151/640   Fat per portion: 0.7 g

—— POACHED NECTARINES ——

550 ml (20 fl oz/2½ cups) unsweetened apple juice
85 g (3 oz/⅓ cup) caster sugar
pared rind of 1 lemon
1 cinnamon stick
8 cloves
4 nectarines
25 g (1 oz/¼ cup) flaked almonds, toasted

In a saucepan, mix together apple juice, sugar, lemon rind, cinnamon stick and cloves. To peel nectarines, dip into boiling water for about 15 seconds, then plunge into a bowl of cold water. Lift nectarines out of the water and peel off skins with a sharp knife.

Add nectarines to juice mixture in saucepan as soon as they are peeled to prevent discolouring. Over a high heat, bring mixture to the boil. Reduce heat to low, cover and simmer for 5-10 minutes, shaking pan occasionally. Spoon nectarines and juice mixture into a bowl. Cool, cover and refrigerate overnight.

Remove cinnamon stick, and rind and cloves if wished, from the juice before serving. To serve, place nectarines and some juice in individual dishes and sprinkle each nectarine with some flaked almonds.

Serves 4.

Total Cals/Kj: 942/3998   Total Fat: 15.0 g
Cals/Kj per portion: 236/999   Fat per portion: 3.7 g

Variation: If nectarines are not available, peaches may be used instead.

———— BLACKBERRY SUPREME ————

450 g (1 lb) blackberries
55 g (2 oz/¼ cup) caster sugar
3 teaspoons powdered gelatine
425 ml (15 fl oz/1¾ cups) low fat fromage frais
fresh blackberries and mint sprigs, to decorate

Place blackberries and sugar in a saucepan with 2 tablespoons water. Cook gently until blackberries have softened. Set aside to cool.

Sprinkle gelatine over 3 tablespoons water in a small bowl and leave for 2-3 minutes to soften. Stand bowl in a saucepan of hot water and stir until gelatine has dissolved. Cool slightly.

In a blender or food processor, purée together blackberries and fromage frais, then stir in gelatine until well mixed. Pour into a large serving dish and chill in the refrigerator until set. Decorate with fresh blackberries and mint sprigs before serving.

Serves 4.

Total Cals/Kj: 884/3787   Total fat: 34.9 g
Cals/Kj per portion: 221/947   Fat per portion: 8.7 g

——CITRUS FRUIT COCKTAIL——

6 oranges
2 pink grapefruit
1 grapefruit
8 kumquats
425 ml (15 fl oz/1¾ cups) freshly squeezed
   orange juice
9 teaspoons clear honey
grated rind of 1 lime
chopped fresh mint or grated lemon or lime rind, to
   decorate (optional)

To prepare fruit, cut off peel and pith from oranges and grapefruit.

Cut out segments from between membranes of fruit holding them over a bowl and place in the bowl. Squeeze membranes over bowl to extract juice. Wipe and thinly slice kumquats crosswise. Place in bowl.

In a measuring jug, mix together orange juice, honey and lime rind. Pour over fruit in the bowl and mix gently to combine. Place in a serving dish and chill in the refrigerator before serving. Serve decorated with chopped fresh mint or lemon or lime rind, if wished.

Serves 4.

Total Cals/Kj: 920/3941   Total fat: 2.9 g
Cals/Kj per portion: 230/985   Fat per portion: 0.7 g

—RASPBERRY APPLE STREUSEL—

450 g (1 lb) cooking apples
350 g (12 oz) raspberries
85 g (3 oz/½ cup) soft brown sugar
85 g (3 oz/⅓ cup) low fat spread
85 g (3 oz/¾ cup) plain wholemeal flour
85 g (3 oz/1 cup) rolled oats
1 teaspoon ground cinnamon

Preheat oven to 200C (400F/Gas 6). Peel, core and slice apples. Place in a saucepan with 2 tablespoons water and cook over a low heat until just softened.

Stir in raspberries and 25 g (1 oz/2 table-spoons) sugar. Place apple mixture in a 1.2 litre (40 fl oz/5 cup) ovenproof dish, keeping back any excess juice. In a bowl, rub together remaining sugar, low fat spread and flour until mixture resembles coarse crumbs. Stir in oats and cinnamon.

Spoon streusel mixture over fruit and press down lightly. Bake in oven for 35-40 minutes until streusel is golden brown and crisp. Serve hot or cold with low fat custard or reduced fat cream.

Serves 6.

Total Cals/Kj: 1455/6121   Total fat: 43.8 g
Cals/Kj per portion: 243/1020   Fat per portion: 7.3 g

—RHUBARB & ORANGE FOOL—

1 kg (2 lb) rhubarb, cut into 2.5 cm (1 in) lengths
6 tablespoons unsweetened orange juice
15 teaspoons strawberry jam
6 teaspoons thick honey
150 ml (5 fl oz/²⁄₃ cup) reduced fat double
    (heavy) cream
300 ml (10 fl oz/1 ¼ cups) Greek yogurt
orange slices and mint sprigs, to decorate

Put rhubarb into a saucepan with orange juice, jam and honey. Bring to the boil, cover and simmer gently until rhubarb is soft and pulpy.

Cool slightly, then purée in a blender or food processor. Turn into a bowl and cool completely. In a separate bowl, whip cream lightly. Fold cream and yogurt into cooled rhubarb mixture.

Spoon mixture into 6 individual glasses and chill in the refrigerator until ready to serve. Decorate each dessert with orange slices and mint sprigs, and serve with sponge fingers.

Serves 6.

Total Cals/Kj: 1066/4487   Total fat: 59.9 g
Cals/Kj per portion: 178/748   Fat per portion: 9.9 g

—RICE & HONEY TABLE CREAM—

9 teaspoons cornflour
550 ml (20 fl oz/2½ cups) skimmed milk
55 g (2 oz/¼ cup) short grain white rice
9 teaspoons thick honey
cocoa powder, to decorate

In a bowl, blend cornflour with 2 tablespoons milk. In a saucepan, gently heat together remaining milk, rice and honey until boiling. Cover and cook slowly for 30 minutes until rice is soft, stirring occasionally.

Pour onto cornflour mixture, stirring well. Return mixture to saucepan and heat until mixture thickens. Cook for a further 3 minutes. Pour into a wetted 685 ml (24 fl oz/ 3 cup) mould and leave to set.

Chill in the refrigerator until ready to serve. To serve, turn out of mould onto a serving dish and sprinkle with sifted cocoa powder. Serve with strawberries, if wished.

Serves 4.

Total Cals/Kj: 683/2898   Total fat: 2.7 g
Cals/Kj per portion: 171/725   Fat per portion: 0.6 g

Note: Make the table cream in four 175 ml (6 fl oz/¾ cup) individual moulds, if preferred.

──────── BAKEWELL TART ────────

225 g (8 oz/2 cups) self-raising flour
115 g (4 oz/½ cup) low fat spread
12 teaspoons reduced sugar raspberry jam
55 g (2 oz/¼ cup) caster sugar
1 egg, beaten
45 g (1½ oz) ground almonds
1 teaspoon almond essence
6 teaspoons icing sugar

Preheat oven to 180C (350F/Gas 4). Sieve
115 g (4 oz/1 cup) flour into a bowl and rub in
55 g (2 oz/¼ cup) low fat spread until mixture
resembles breadcrumbs.

Add enough water to make a soft dough. On
a lightly floured surface, roll out pastry and
use to line a 20 cm (8 in) flan dish. Prick base
of pastry with a fork. Bake blind in oven for
10 minutes. Cool slightly, then spread with
raspberry jam. In a bowl, cream together
remaining low fat spread and sugar. Gradually add egg and beat well. Fold in remaining
flour, ground almonds and essence. Spoon
it over the jam, levelling the surface. Bake in
the oven for 25 minutes until golden brown.

In a small bowl, mix icing sugar with 2 tablespoons water and spread over tart while still
warm. Serve warm or cold.

Serves 8.

Total Cals/Kj: 1980/8451   Total fat: 82.6 g
Cals/Kj per portion: 248/1056   Fat per portion: 10.3 g

Note: Add a few drops of red food colouring
to half of the icing and dribble over the white
icing to give a feathered effect.

──── QUICK CHERRY BRÛLÉE ────

400 g (14 oz) can cherries
300 ml (10 fl oz/1¼ cups) Greek yogurt
55 g (2 oz/⅓ cup) soft brown sugar
mint sprigs, to decorate

Drain and the stone cherries. Place them in an 850 ml (30 fl oz/3¾ cup) ovenproof dish.

Spread the Greek yogurt over the cherries and sprinkle the sugar over the yogurt, covering it completely.

Put under a preheated medium grill until sugar becomes dark and bubbling. Leave to cool, then chill in the refrigerator for 2-3 hours. Serve decorated with mint sprigs.

Serves 4.

Total Cals/Kj: 827/3501	Total fat: 22.5 g
Cals/Kj per portion: 207/875	Fat per portion: 5.6 g

— LOGANBERRY LAYER DESSERT —

225 g (8 oz) loganberries
225 ml (8 fl oz/1 cup) reduced fat double
   (heavy) cream
550 ml (20 fl oz/2½ cups) very low fat fromage frais
55 g (2 oz/½ cup) icing sugar, sifted
fresh loganberries and herb sprigs, to decorate

Place loganberries in a saucepan with 2 tablespoons water. Cook gently until just softened. Cool slightly, then purée in a blender or food processor. Cool completely. In a bowl, whip cream until thick.

In a separate bowl, gently mix together puréed loganberries, half the cream, half the fromage frais and 25 g (1 oz/¼ cup) icing sugar. In another bowl, gently mix together remaining cream, fromage frais and icing sugar.

Layer loganberry mixture and fromage frais mixture in 6 glasses, finishing with a loganberry layer. Chill in the refrigerator until ready to serve. Decorate desserts with fresh loganberries and herb sprigs before serving.

Serves 6.

Total Cals/Kj: 1238/5226   Total fat: 56.4 g
Cals/Kj per portion: 206/871   Fat per portion: 9.4 g

—— SPICED APPLE PUDDING ——

225 g (8 oz) cooking apples
115 g (4 oz/½ cup) low fat spread
85 g (3 oz/½ cup) soft brown sugar
2 eggs
175 g (6 oz/1½ cups) self-raising flour
115 g (4 oz/¾ cup) sultanas
2 tablespoons skimmed milk

Preheat oven to 180C (350F/Gas 4). Peel, core and roughly chop apples. In a bowl, cream low fat spread and sugar together until light and fluffy.

Beat eggs in a separate small bowl, then beat into the creamed mixture, a little at a time. Sift flour into mixture and fold in, using a metal spoon. Add apples, sultanas and milk and mix thoroughly.

Spoon mixture into a greased 1.2 litre (40 fl oz/5 cup) ovenproof dish. Bake in oven for 1 hour until golden brown on top. Serve hot, with low fat yogurt sprinkled with cinnamon or low fat custard.

Serves 8.

Total Cals/Kj: 1977/8334   Total fat: 65.6 g
Cals/Kj per portion: 247/1042   Fat per portion: 8.2 g

——— BRAMBLE JELLY RING ———

225 g (8 oz) blackberries
225 g (8 oz) raspberries
55 g (2 oz/¼ cup) caster sugar
5 teaspoons powdered gelatine
300 ml (10 fl oz/1¼ cups) unsweetened apple juice
fresh berries and herb sprigs, to decorate

Place blackberries and raspberries in a saucepan with 300 ml (10 fl oz/1¼ cups) water and
the sugar. Simmer over a low heat until soft.
Allow to cool.

Purée fruit mixture in a blender or food processor, then press through sieve, until all the
juice has been extracted. Discard pips.
Sprinkle gelatine over 3 tablespoons water in
a small bowl and leave for 2-3 minutes to
soften. Stand bowl in a saucepan of hot water
and stir until gelatine has dissolved. Cool
slightly.

Stir gelatine into fruit juice mixture with
apple juice. Mix well and pour into a wetted
850 ml (30 fl oz/3¾ cup) ring mould. Chill in
the refrigerator until set. To serve, turn out of
mould and decorate with fresh berries and
herb sprigs.

Serves 4.

Total Cals/Kj: 508/2253   Total fat: 1.3 g
Cals/Kj per portion: 127/563   Fat per portion: 0.3 g

─────── MOCHA WHIP ───────

55 g (2 oz) plain (dark) chocolate
½ teaspoon instant coffee granules
3 teaspoons powdered gelatine
300 ml (10 fl oz/1 ¼ cups) very low fat fromage frais
300 ml (10 fl oz/1 ¼ cups) low fat fromage frais
6 teaspoons clear honey
115 g (4 oz) trifle sponge cakes, broken roughly
 into pieces
fresh fruit and chocolate vermicelli, to decorate

Break chocolate into pieces and melt in a
bowl set over a pan of simmering water.
Allow to cool. Dissolve coffee granules in
1 tablespoon warm water.

Sprinkle gelatine over 3 tablespoons water in
a small bowl and leave for 2-3 minutes to
soften. Stand bowl in a saucepan of hot water
and stir until gelatine has dissolved. Allow to
cool. In a bowl, mix together chocolate,
coffee, gelatine, fromage frais and honey
until thoroughly combined. If, at this stage,
mixture begins to harden, place bowl over a
saucepan of hot water for a few minutes until
mixture softens again.

Layer mocha mixture and trifle sponge cakes
in individual glass dishes or one large glass
serving dish, finishing with a mocha layer.
Chill in the refrigerator until set. To serve,
decorate with fresh fruit and chocolate
vermicelli.

Serves 6.

Total Cals/Kj: 1310/5509   Total fat: 47.5 g
Cals/Kj per portion: 218/918   Fat per portion: 7.9 g

— SPICY DRIED FRUIT COMPOTE —

300 g (10 oz) mixed dried fruit salad, such as apricots,
   apples, prunes, pears, peaches, figs
300 ml (10 fl oz/1¼ cups) unsweetened orange juice
1 teaspoon ground mixed spice
25 g (1 oz/¼ cup) flaked almonds, toasted

Place dried fruit in a serving dish. In a
measuring jug, mix together orange juice and
mixed spice with 300 ml (10 fl oz/1¼ cups)
water.

Pour juice over mixed dried fruit and stir well
to combine. Cover and leave to soak in the
refrigerator overnight.

When ready to serve, sprinkle flaked almonds
over the top of the fruit and serve with Greek
yogurt, if wished.

Serves 4.

Total Cals/Kj: 862/3654   Total fat: 15.8 g
Cals/Kj per portion: 216/914   Fat per portion: 3.9 g

CAROB FRUIT PIZZA

100 g (3½ oz/⅓ cup) low fat spread
55 g (2 oz/¼ cup) caster sugar
150 g (5 oz/1¼ cups) plain flour
20 g (¾ oz/6 teaspoons) carob flour
150 ml (5 fl oz/⅔ cup) reduced fat double
  (heavy) cream
225 g (8 oz) fresh fruit, such as strawberries,
  raspberries, blackberries, grapes, redcurrants

Preheat oven to 160C (325F/Gas 3). In a
bowl, cream together the low fat spread and
sugar until light and fluffy. Sift flour and
carob flour into mixture and fold in using a
metal spoon until mixture binds together.
Knead well to form a smooth dough.

On a lightly floured surface, roll out dough to
a 20 cm (8 in) round. Place on a greased
baking sheet and flute the edges of the dough
to make an attractive base. Bake in oven for
30 minutes.

Remove from oven and place on a wire rack
to cool. To serve, whip cream stiffly. Spread
it over the carob base and top with fresh fruit.
Serve immediately.

Serves 8.

Total Cals/Kj: 1567/6653   Total fat: 79.0 g
Cals/Kj per portion: 196/832   Fat per portion: 9.8 g

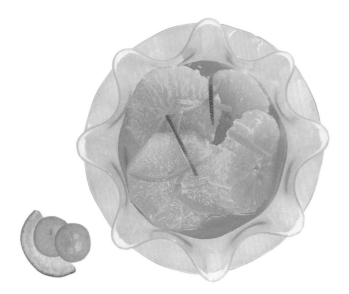

GLAZED ORANGES

4 large oranges
55 g (2 oz/⅓ cup) soft brown sugar
6 teaspoons Cointreau or orange liqueur
grated lime or orange rind, to decorate

Grate rind from one orange. Set aside. Peel all the oranges and slice thickly.

Place orange slices in a saucepan with 550 ml (20 fl oz/2½ cups) water, sugar and grated orange rind. Heat gently over a low heat until mixture is boiling, then simmer for 5 minutes. Remove from heat.

Add Cointreau and stir gently to combine. Place in a serving dish, allow to cool, then refrigerate overnight before serving. Decorate with grated lime or orange rind, if wished. Serve with reduced fat cream or low fat plain yogurt, if wished.

Serves 4.

Total Cals/Kj: 442/1884   Total fat: 0.5 g
Cals/Kj per portion: 111/471   Fat per portion: 0.1 g

TROPICAL CHOUX RING

55 g (2 oz/¼ cup) butter
70 g (2½ oz/½ cup) plain flour, sifted
2 eggs, beaten
400 ml (14 fl oz/1¾ cups) low fat ready-made
   cold custard
225 g (8 oz) pineapple, peeled, cored and chopped
1 medium papaya, peeled, seeds removed and chopped
2 kiwi fruit, peeled and chopped
1 carambola (starfruit), sliced
2 tablespoons icing sugar

Preheat oven to 200C (400F/Gas 6). Place butter in a saucepan with 150 ml (5 fl oz/ ⅔ cup) water. Heat gently until fat has melted, then bring mixture to the boil.

Remove saucepan from heat. Add flour to hot mixture and beat thoroughly with a wooden spoon. Beat mixture until it is smooth and forms a ball in the centre of the pan. Allow mixture to cool slightly, then gradually add eggs, beating well after each addition, until pastry dough is smooth and shiny. Drop tablespoons of dough onto a greased baking sheet to form a ring. Bake in oven for 40 minutes until risen and golden brown. Remove from oven carefully, transfer to a wire rack and immediately slice ring horizontally in half to release steam inside.

Allow to cool completely. In a bowl, gently mix together custard and prepared fruit. Spoon fruit mixture onto bottom of pastry ring. Replace top of pastry ring. Sprinkle with sifted icing sugar to serve.

Serves 8.

Total Cals/Kj: 1554/6569   Total fat: 64.7 g
Cals/Kj per portion: 194/821   Fat per portion: 8.0 g

Note: Place the tablespoons of dough so that they are just touching on the baking sheet.

— FOREST FRUITS CHEESECAKE —

45 g (1½ oz) low fat spread
115 g (4 oz) semi-sweet wheatmeal biscuits, crushed
225 g (8 oz) mixed berries, such as raspberries,
   strawberries, blackberries, black-and redcurrants
3 teaspoons powdered gelatine
115 g (4 oz/½ cup) skimmed milk soft cheese
45 g (1½ oz/9 teaspoons) caster sugar
150 ml (5 fl oz/⅔ cup) very low fat fromage frais
150 ml (5 fl oz/⅔ cup) reduced fat double
   (heavy) cream
1 tablespoon reduced sugar blackcurrant jam
fresh mixed berries, to decorate

Melt low fat spread in a saucepan over a low
heat. Mix in biscuit crumbs.

Press mixture into a 20 cm (8 in) loose-
bottomed tin, so that it covers the base.
Chill. Place mixed berries in a saucepan with
3 tablespoons water and simmer gently until
soft. Cool completely. Sprinkle gelatine over
3 tablespoons water in a small bowl and leave
for 2-3 minutes to soften. Place bowl over a
saucepan of hot water and stir until dissolved.
Leave to cool slightly. Place soft cheese,
sugar, fromage frais, cream, cooked fruit, jam
and gelatine in a food processor or blender
and blend until smooth.

Pour onto biscuit base and chill in the
refrigerator until set. To serve, remove from
tin, place on a serving plate and decorate
with mixed berries.

Serves 8.

Total Cals/Kj: 1542/6524   Total fat: 78.6 g
Cals/Kj per portion: 193/816   Fat per portion: 9.8 g

Note: To crush biscuits easily, place them in
a large plastic bag and roll over the bag with a
rolling pin until biscuits are crushed.

——— PLUM CUSTARD TART ———

450 g (1 lb) plums or damsons
55 g (2 oz/½ cup) plain flour
55 g (2 oz/½ cup) wholemeal plain flour
55 g (2 oz/¼ cup) low fat spread
300 ml (10 fl oz/1¼ cups) skimmed milk
2 eggs
55 g (2 oz/¼ cup) caster sugar
few drops almond essence

Preheat oven to 180C (350F/Gas 4). Wash and drain plums or damsons; set aside. Sift flours into a bowl and rub in low fat spread until mixture resembles breadcrumbs.

Add enough water to make a soft dough. On a lightly floured surface, roll out pastry and use to line a 20 cm (8 in) flan dish. Prick base of pastry with a fork. Bake blind in oven for 10 minutes. Place plums or damsons in base of pastry case.

In a bowl, beat together milk, eggs, sugar and almond essence. Pour over plums or damsons. Bake in oven for 45 minutes until custard is set and golden. Serve warm or cold.

Serves 6.

Total Cals/Kj: 1253/5367   Total fat: 40.6 g
Cals/Kj per portion: 209/895   Fat per portion: 6.7 g

Note: Almond essence is strong in flavour – use it sparingly.

GREEN FRUIT SALAD

½ honeydew melon
3 kiwi fruit
2 green-skinned eating apples
2 pears
300 g (10 oz) green seedless grapes
425 ml (15 fl oz/1¾ cups) white grape juice
6 teaspoons clear honey
mint sprigs, to decorate

To prepare fruit, peel and remove seeds from melon and cut flesh into chunks.

Peel kiwi fruit and cut into chunks. Core apples and pears, then cut into chunks. Halve grapes if large in size. Place fruit in a large serving dish. In a measuring jug, mix together grape juice and honey.

Pour juice over fruit and mix gently to combine. Chill in the refrigerator before serving. Serve decorated with mint sprigs.

Serves 6.

Total Cals/Kj: 929/3968   Total fat: 2.4 g
Cals/Kj per portion: 155/661   Fat per portion: 0.4 g

Variation: Use apple juice instead of white grape juice for a change.

– PEAR & CINNAMON CRUMBLE –

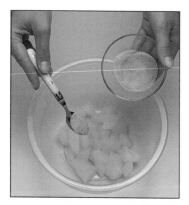

two 400 g (14 oz) cans pear halves in fruit juice
3 teaspoons caster sugar
2 teaspoons ground cinnamon
150 g (5 oz/1¼ cups) plain wholemeal flour
55 g (2 oz/⅓ cup) soft brown sugar
85 g (3 oz/⅓ cup) low fat spread

Preheat oven to 200C (400F/Gas 6). Drain
pears, reserving juice, and chop roughly. Mix
caster sugar with 1 teaspoon cinnamon and
mix with pears.

In a bowl, mix together remaining cinnamon, flour and sugar. Rub in low fat spread
until mixture resembles breadcrumbs.

In a 1.2 litre (40 fl oz/5 cup) ovenproof dish,
layer crumble mixture and pear mixture,
pouring pear juice over fruit, finishing with a
crumble layer. Bake in oven for 30 minutes
until golden brown on top. Serve hot or cold
with low fat custard or reduced fat cream.

Serves 6.

Total Cals/Kj: 1339/5673   Total fat: 38.0 g
Cals/Kj per portion: 223/946   Fat per portion: 6.3 g

LEMON ORANGE CUPS

4 large oranges
grated rind of 1 lemon
150 ml (5 fl oz/²/₃ cup) reduced fat double
   (heavy) cream
115 g (4 oz/¹/₂ cup) low fat soft cheese
julienne strips of lemon and orange rind, to decorate

Cut each orange in half crosswise. Remove flesh and chop finely, then place in a bowl. Drain shells upside down on a wire rack.

Mix lemon rind and chopped orange flesh together. Whip cream lightly and mix with soft cheese. Add cheese mixture to chopped oranges and stir gently to mix. Thinly slice base off each orange shell so that they will sit level.

Fill all the shells with orange and cheese mixture and place on a serving plate. Any cheese mixture left over can be served separately alongside desserts. Chill in the refrigerator until ready to serve. Decorate with lemon and orange rind before serving.

Serves 8.

Total Cals/Kj: 813/3419   Total fat: 44.9 g
Cals/Kj per portion: 102/427   Fat per portion: 5.6 g

——— SUMMER PUDDING ———

225 g (8 oz) blackcurrants
115 g (4 oz) redcurrants
115 g (4 oz) loganberries
115 g (4 oz) strawberries
115 g (4 oz) raspberries
115 g (4 oz) blackberries
2 tablespoons clear honey
8 medium slices wholemeal bread

Place fruit and honey in a saucepan with 3 tablespoons water. Bring mixture slowly to the boil and cook over a low heat until juicy. Cut crusts off bread and cut bread into strips.

Line a 1.25 litre (40 fl oz/5 cup) pudding basin with three-quarters of the bread. Place fruit in basin and cover with remaining bread. Place a saucer with a weight on it on top of the pudding. Leave to cool, then refrigerate overnight.

To serve, turn pudding out onto a flat plate and serve in wedges with reduced fat cream.

Serves 6.

Total Cals/Kj: 819/3487   Total fat: 6.8 g
Cals/Kj per portion: 137/581   Fat per portion: 1.1 g

Note: White or Granary bread may be used in place of wholemeal bread. Decorate the top of the pudding with redcurrants dipped in sugar syrup and coated with sugar, if wished.

MIXED GRAPE TARTLETS

85 g (3 oz/¾ cup) plain flour
1 teaspoon caster sugar
55 g (2 oz/¼ cup) low fat spread
150 ml (5 fl oz/⅔ cup) low fat ready-made cold custard
85 g (3 oz) seedless green grapes
85 g (3 oz) seedless black grapes
9 teaspoons reduced sugar apricot jam, warmed

Preheat oven to 190C (375F/Gas 5). Sift flour into a bowl and mix in sugar. Rub low fat spread into flour until mixture resembles breadcrumbs. Add enough water to make a soft dough.

On a lightly floured surface, roll out dough and, with a 7.5 cm (3 in) fluted cutter, cut out 12 rounds. Use pastry rounds to line 12 patty tins. Prick bases of pastry rounds with a fork. Bake blind in oven for 12-15 minutes until golden brown.

Cool tartlet cases in tin for 10 minutes, then remove from tin and place on a wire rack. Cool completely. Place a spoonful of custard into each tartlet case and arrange grapes on top. Brush with warmed apricot jam to glaze before serving.

Makes 12.

Cals/Kj per tartlet: 67/283   Fat per tartlet: 2.1 g

——— CITRUS CRUNCH FLAN ———

115 g (4 oz/1 cup) plain flour
55 g (2 oz/⅓ cup) soft brown sugar
55 g (2 oz/¼ cup) low fat spread
25 g (1 oz/¼ cup) chopped mixed nuts
juice and grated rind of 1 lemon
juice and grated rind of 1 orange
4 tablespoons freshly squeezed orange juice
45 g (1½ oz/7 teaspoons) caster sugar
6 teaspoons cornflour
2 eggs, separated
lemon and lime slices, to decorate

Preheat oven to 180C (350F/Gas 4). Sift flour into a bowl. Stir in brown sugar and rub in low fat spread until resembles breadcrumbs.

Stir in nuts and mix well. Press crumble mixture lightly onto base of a 20 cm (8 in) flan tin. To make filling, place fruit juices in a measuring jug and make up to 300 ml (10 fl oz/1¼ cups) with water. In a saucepan, blend together caster sugar, cornflour and 2 tablespoons fruit juice. Add remaining fruit juice, grated rinds and egg yolks and heat gently, stirring continuously, until mixture thickens. Leave to cool for 10 minutes, stirring occasionally to prevent lumps forming.

In a bowl, whisk egg whites stiffly. Gradually fold into fruit custard. Pour custard over crumble base. Bake in oven for 30-45 minutes, until golden brown. Leave in flan tin to cool, then chill in the refrigerator. Decorate with lemon and lime slices. Serve chilled, with reduced fat cream.

Serves 6.

Total Cals/Kj: 1491/6350   Total fat: 53.5 g
Cals/Kj per portion: 248/1058   Fat per portion: 8.9 g

——— STRAWBERRY CHIFFON ———

400 g (14 oz) can strawberries in fruit juice
3 teaspoons powdered gelatine
300 ml (10 fl oz/1¼ cups) reduced fat evaporated milk
300 ml (10 fl oz/1¼ cups) skimmed milk
150 ml (5 fl oz/⅔ cup) low fat plain yogurt
1 tablespoon clear honey
strawberry slices, to decorate

Drain juice from strawberries into a bowl and make up to 300 ml (10 fl oz/1¼ cups) with water.

Put 4 tablespoons strawberry juice into a small bowl and sprinkle on gelatine. Leave for 2-3 minutes to soften. Place bowl over a saucepan of hot water and stir until dissolved. Allow to cool slightly, then pour into remaining juice, mix well and cool until on the point of setting. In a bowl, whisk evaporated milk until thick. Gradually add half the strawberries, gelatine mixture and milk and pour into a serving dish. Leave to set in the refrigerator. Whisk remaining strawberries into the yogurt and honey and mix well.

Serve chiffon in portions with yogurt sauce poured over. Decorate with strawberries.

Serves 6.

Total Cals/Kj: 710/2994   Total fat: 13.8 g
Cals/Kj per portion: 118/499   Fat per portion: 2.3 g

Note: When combining whipped evaporated milk with a gelatine mixture, it is essential that the base mixture is on the point of setting, otherwise the mixture will separate out to jelly on the bottom and froth on the top.

— KIWI & GRAPE SPONGE FLAN —

2 eggs
55 g (2 oz/¼ cup) caster sugar
55 g (2 oz/½ cup) plain flour
175 g (6 oz) green grapes
2 kiwi fruit
9 teaspoons reduced sugar apricot jam

Preheat oven to 180C (350F/Gas 4). Grease a 20 cm (8 in) raised-base flan tin. In a bowl, whisk together eggs and sugar until mixture is very thick. Sift flour into mixture and fold in gently with a metal spoon.

Turn into prepared tin and level the surface. Bake in the oven for 20-25 minutes, until light golden brown. Turn out onto a wire rack and leave to cool. Halve and seed the grapes and peel and slice the kiwi fruit.

Arrange fruit in flan case. In a saucepan, gently heat jam with 1 tablespoon water. Cool slightly, then brush over the fruit to glaze. Serve with low fat custard or reduced fat cream.

Serves 6.

Total Cals/Kj: 827/3585   Total fat: 17.6 g
Cals/Kj per portion: 138/598   Fat per portion: 2.9 g

——BLACKBERRY MILK JELLY——

225 g (8 oz) blackberries
55 g (2 oz/¼ cup) caster sugar
3 teaspoons powdered gelatine
550 ml (20 fl oz/2½ cups) semi-skimmed milk
fresh blackberries and mint sprig, to decorate

Place blackberries and sugar in a saucepan with 1 tablespoon water and cook gently until soft. Allow to cool, then purée in a blender or food processor and cool completely.

Sprinkle gelatine over 3 tablespoons water in a small bowl. Leave for 2-3 minutes to soften. Place bowl in a saucepan of hot water and stir until dissolved. Allow to cool slightly. Mix into blackberry purée. In a bowl, mix together fruit purée and milk and stir well. Pour into a wetted 850 ml (30 fl oz/3¾ cup) mould.

Chill in the refrigerator until set. To serve, turn out mould onto a serving plate and decorate with fresh blackberries and mint.

Serves 4.

Total Cals/Kj: 557/2446   Total fat: 9.2 g
Cals/Kj per portion: 139/612 Fat per portion: 2.3 g

Note: The blackberry mixture must be completely cool before combining with the milk to prevent the mixture curdling.

—— PINEAPPLE FRUIT BOATS ——

1 large pineapple
225 g (8 oz) strawberries
2 peaches
175 g (6 oz) fresh dates
55 g (2 oz/½ cup) chopped hazelnuts
mint sprigs, to decorate

Cut pineapple in half lengthwise. Cut out core and chunks of flesh. Cut a thin slice from underneath, so that the pineapple halves sit flat.

Halve strawberries. Peel, stone and chop peaches. Stone dates and cut into quarters. In a bowl, mix together pineapple flesh and other fruits, then pile into the pineapple boats.

Sprinkle each pineapple fruit boat with chopped hazelnuts and serve, decorated with mint sprigs.

Serves 6.

Total Cals/Kj: 1038/4344   Total fat: 37.0 g
Cals/Kj per portion: 173/724   Fat per portion: 6.1 g

Note: Top pineapple boats with Greek yogurt just before serving, if wished.

—BANANA & GINGER BRÛLÉE—

350 ml (12 fl oz/1½ cups) reduced fat single
  (light) cream
150 ml (5 fl oz/⅔ cup) reduced fat double
  (heavy) cream
4 egg yolks
85 g (3 oz/⅓ cup) caster sugar
2 large bananas
2 teaspoons ground ginger

Preheat oven to 150C (300F/Gas 2). In a
saucepan, heat warm creams together until
almost boiling. In a bowl, beat together egg
yolks and 55 g (2 oz/¼ cup) sugar until pale.
Gradually pour cream mixture onto egg
mixture, whisking.

Stand 8 small ramekin dishes in an ovenproof
dish, or dishes, and pour enough water into
ovenproof dish so that it comes 1 cm (½ in)
up the sides of the ramekins. Peel and slice
bananas thinly and place some banana slices
in base of each ramekin. Sprinkle ginger
over bananas. Pour custard mixture over the
bananas.

Bake in oven for 1 hour until golden brown
on top. Allow to cool, then refrigerate.
Sprinkle remaining sugar over desserts and
place under a medium grill until the sugar
melts and turns brown. Cool, then chill.

Serves 8.

Total Cals/Kj: 1520/6506   Total fat: 84.0 g
Cals/Kj per portion: 190/813   Fat per portion: 10.5 g

Note: Decorate with mint sprigs and fruit,
if wished.

–NECTARINE MERINGUE NESTS–

3 egg whites
175 g (6 oz/¾ cup) caster sugar
115 g (4 oz/½ cup) skimmed milk soft cheese
150 ml (5 fl oz/⅔ cup) low fat fromage frais
3 nectarines
115 g (4 oz) blackcurrants
6 teaspoons reduced sugar apricot jam

Preheat oven to 150C (300F/Gas 2). Line a large baking sheet with non-stick baking parchment. In a large bowl, whisk egg whites stiffly. Gradually add sugar, beating well after each addition, until mixture is stiff and glossy.

Spoon meringue into a piping bag fitted with a star nozzle and pipe meringue in six 10 cm (4 in) rounds onto the lined baking sheet, leaving a gap between them. Pipe remaining meringue in stars around the edge of each round to form an attractive border. Bake meringue nests in oven for 1-1½ hours until crisp on the outside. Cool on a wire rack. In a bowl, stir together soft cheese and fromage frais, mixing well. Peel and stone nectarines and slice thinly. Top and tail blackcurrants, wash and drain.

In a saucepan, gently heat apricot jam with 1 tablespoon water until warm. To fill each meringue nest, place some cheese mixture in the nest. Top with sliced nectarines and blackcurrants, then brush with warmed jam to glaze. Refrigerate until ready to serve.

Serves 6.

Total Cals/Kj: 1205/5379   Total fat: 12.5 g
Cals/Kj per portion: 201/897   Fat per portion: 2.0 g

FRUITY FILO PARCELS

1 eating apple
2 teaspoons lemon juice
2 kiwi fruit
1 peach
55 g (2 oz/⅓ cup) raisins
1 teaspoon ground mixed spice
8 sheets filo pastry
55 g (2 oz/¼ cup) low fat spread, melted
1 tablespoon icing sugar
strawberry slices, to decorate (optional)

Preheat oven to 200C (400F/Gas 6). To prepare filling, peel, core and coarsely grate apple into a bowl and sprinkle with lemon juice to prevent discoloration.

Peel kiwi fruit, chop roughly and add to apple. Peel, stone and chop peach roughly and add to apple with raisins and mixed spice. Stir well to mix. Set aside. To make each filo parcel, cut each filo sheet in half crosswise to make two 10 cm (4 in) squares (total of 16 squares). Brush 2 squares of pastry lightly with melted fat, then place one on top of the other diagonally. Place some fruit filling in the centre of the pastry and then fold over all the sides like a parcel.

Place seam-edge downwards onto a greased baking sheet and brush lightly with melted fat. Repeat with remaining pastry squares and filling, to make 8 parcels. Bake in oven for 30 minutes until golden brown and crisp. Sprinkle with sifted icing sugar just before serving and decorate with a few slices of strawberry, if wished. Serve hot or cold.

Makes 8.

Cals/Kj per parcel: 135/569   Fat per parcel: 3.5 g

— MIXED CURRANT SENSATION —

115 g (4 oz) blackcurrants
115 g (4 oz) redcurrants
115 g (4 oz) white currants
3 teaspoons thick honey
3 teaspoons powdered gelatine
400 ml (14 fl oz/1¾ cups) low fat ready-made
   cold custard
300 ml (10 fl oz/1¼ cups) reduced fat single
   (light) cream
25 g (1 oz/¼ cup) mixed chopped nuts

Reserve a few currants for decoration. Put remaining currants in a saucepan with honey and 2 tablespoons water. Heat gently until just soft. Leave to cool completely.

Sprinkle gelatine over 3 tablespoons water in a small bowl and leave for 2-3 minutes to soften. Place bowl in a saucepan of hot water and stir until dissolved. Cool. Place currants and juice, gelatine, custard and cream in a blender or food processor and purée until well mixed.

Pour mixture into individual serving dishes and leave to set in the refrigerator. When ready to serve, sprinkle chopped nuts over each dessert and decorate with the reserved currants. Serve chilled.

Serves 6.

Total Cals/Kj: 1042/4372   Total fat: 47.6 g
Cals/Kj per portion: 174/728   Fat per portion: 7.9 g

Note: Desserts set more quickly if placed in a container full of cold water and ice cubes.

───── FRENCH APPLE TART ─────

115 g (4 oz/1 cup) plain flour
1 teaspoon caster sugar
85 g (3 oz/⅓ cup) low fat spread
1 kg (2 lb) cooking apples
grated rind and juice of 1 lemon
4 tablespoons reduced sugar apricot jam
225 g (8 oz) eating apples

Preheat oven to 180C (350F/Gas 4). Sift
flour into a bowl and mix in the sugar. Rub in
55 g (2 oz/¼ cup) of the low fat spread until
mixture resembles breadcrumbs. Add enough
water to make a soft dough. On a lightly
floured surface, roll out the dough.

Use dough to line a 20 cm (8 in) loose-
bottomed flan tin. Prick base of pastry all
over with a fork. Bake blind in oven for 10
minutes. Peel, core and slice cooking apples
and place in a saucepan with remaining low
fat spread and 2 tablespoons water. Cover
and cook gently for 15 minutes, until apples
are soft. Add grated lemon rind and 3 tablespoons jam. Cook for a further 15 minutes
until purée has thickened. Spoon apple
purée into flan case and leave to cool. Peel,
core and slice eating apples thinly.

Arrange in an overlapping circle around edge
of flan and in the centre. Brush with lemon
juice. Bake in oven for 30-40 minutes until
light brown on top. Warm remaining jam and
brush over flan to glaze. Serve warm or cold
with low fat custard or reduced fat cream
sprinkled with cinnamon.

Serves 6.

Total Cals/Kj: 1173/4929   Total fat: 36.9 g
Cals/Kj per portion: 196/822   Fat per portion: 6.1 g

──ORCHARD FRUIT SALAD──

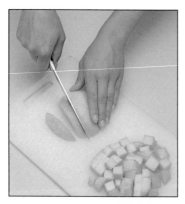

300 g (10 oz) lychees
1 medium mango
2 firm bananas
6 red dessert plums
2 pears
2 Cox's eating apples
1 carambola (starfruit)
300 ml (10 fl oz/1¼ cups) unsweetened apple juice
150 ml (5 fl oz/⅔ cup) dry sherry

To prepare fruit, peel lychees, halve and remove stones. Peel mango, remove stone and cut flesh into chunks.

Peel and slice bananas and halve and stone plums. Core pears and apples and cut flesh into chunks. Slice carambola thinly. Place all the fruit in a large serving dish.

In a separate bowl, mix together apple juice and sherry. Pour over the fruit and stir gently to mix. Chill in the refrigerator overnight before serving. Serve with Greek yogurt.

Serves 6.

Total Cals/Kj: 1106/4715   Total fat: 2.6 g
Cals/Kj per portion: 184/786   Fat per portion: 0.4 g

— PINEAPPLE & RASPBERRY LOG —

3 eggs
85 g (3 oz/⅓ cup) caster sugar
85 g (3 oz/¾ cup) plain flour
1 tablespoon caster sugar
12 teaspoons reduced sugar raspberry jam, warmed
225 g (8 oz) canned pineapple, drained and
   finely chopped
raspberries and mint leaves, to decorate

Preheat oven to 200C (400F/Gas 6). Grease a
32.5 × 22.5 cm (13 × 9 in) Swiss roll tin.
Line with greaseproof paper and grease the
paper.

In a large bowl placed over a pan of hot water,
whisk eggs and sugar until thick and creamy.
Remove bowl from heat and whisk until cool.
Sift half the flour over mixture and fold in
lightly with a metal spoon. Sift and fold in
remaining flour together with 1 tablespoon
hot water. Pour mixture into tin and tilt to
spread the mixture evenly. Bake in oven for
10-12 minutes until risen and golden brown.
Meanwhile, place a sheet of greaseproof
paper over a damp tea towel. Sprinkle paper
with 1 tablespoon caster sugar.

Quickly turn cake onto the paper, trim off
crusty edges and spread with jam. Top with
pineapple and roll up the cake with the aid of
the paper. Place seam-side down on a wire
rack and leave to cool before serving decorated with raspberries and mint leaves.

Serves 6.

Total Cals/Kj: 1159/5054   Total fat: 25.3 g
Cals/Kj per portion: 193/842   Fat per portion: 4.2 g

— GOOSEBERRY YOGURT SNOW —

350 g (12 oz) gooseberries
85 g (3 oz/⅓ cup) caster sugar
425 ml (15 fl oz/1¾ cups) Greek yogurt
mint sprigs, to decorate

Place gooseberries in a saucepan with 2 table-spoons water. Cook gently until soft.

Stir sugar into gooseberries and leave to cool. Purée cooled gooseberries, juice and yogurt in a blender or food processor until smooth.

Pour mixture into 6 serving dishes and chill in the refrigerator before serving. To serve, decorate with mint sprigs.

Serves 6.

Total Cals/Kj: 895/3902   Total fat: 32.8 g
Cals/Kj per portion: 149/650   Fat per portion: 5.4 g

Variation: Bottled gooseberries in syrup may be used instead of fresh gooseberries – omit 55 g (2 oz/¼ cup) caster sugar and blend gooseberries with remaining sugar and yogurt.

— BLUSHING SUMMER FRUITS —

300 ml (10 fl oz/1¼ cups) red wine
85 g (3 oz/⅓ cup) caster sugar
grated rind of 1 lemon
2 red-skinned eating apples
4 dessert plums
225 g (8 oz) strawberries
225 g (8 oz) black grapes
115 g (4 oz) raspberries
lemon slices and rind and mint sprigs, to decorate

Put wine and sugar into a saucepan with grated lemon rind and 300 ml (10 fl oz/1¼ cups) water. Bring to the boil slowly and boil rapidly for 5 minutes.

To prepare fruit, core apples and cut flesh into chunks. Halve and stone plums and halve strawberries. Halve and seed grapes.

Place all the fruit into a serving dish and pour the hot wine mixture over. Stir gently to mix. Leave to cool and serve decorated with lemon slices and rind and mint sprigs.

Serves 6.

Total Cals/Kj: 913/3999   Total fat: 1.0 g
Cals/Kj per portion: 152/667   Fat per portion: 0.1 g

Note: If the fruits are left to soak overnight, they absorb more of the liquor, producing an even more delicious dessert!

——FRESH APRICOT FLAN——

175 g (6 oz/1½ cups) plain flour
85 g (3 oz/⅓ cup) low fat spread
10 fresh apricots
300 ml (10 fl oz/1¼ cups) skimmed milk
2 eggs
45 g (1½ oz/7 teaspoons) caster sugar
1 teaspoon vanilla essence

Preheat oven to 180C (350F/Gas 4). Sift flour into a bowl and rub in low fat spread until mixture resembles breadcrumbs. Add enough water to make a soft dough. On a lightly floured surface, roll out dough and use to line a 20 cm (8 in) loose-bottomed flan tin.

Prick base of pastry all over. Bake blind in oven for 10 minutes. Skin, halve and stone apricots and arrange over the base of the flan case. In a bowl, beat together milk, eggs, sugar and essence.

Pour mixture over apricots. Bake in oven for 30-45 minutes until filling is set and golden brown. Serve warm or cold.

Serves 6.

Total Cals/Kj: 1496/6366   Total fat: 53.2 g
Cals/Kj per portion: 249/1061   Fat per portion: 8.8 g

-FRUITY CHEESECAKE SQUARES-

175 g (6 oz) ginger biscuits or semi-sweet
wheatmeal biscuits
55 g (2 oz/¼ cup) low fat spread, melted
3 teaspoons powdered gelatine
225 g (8 oz/1 cup) cottage cheese
175 g (6 oz/¾ cup) skimmed milk soft cheese
55 g (2 oz/¼ cup) caster sugar
150 ml (5 fl oz/⅔ cup) reduced fat double
   (heavy) cream
grated rind of 1 lemon
225 g (8 oz) strawberries, roughly chopped
kiwi fruit slices, to decorate

Crush biscuits to crumbs and mix with the
melted low fat spread.

Press biscuit crumb mixture over the base of a
17.5 × 25 cm (7 × 10 in) cake tin and chill.
Sprinkle gelatine over 3 tablespoons water in
a small bowl and leave for 2-3 minutes to
soften. Place bowl in a saucepan of hot water
and stir until dissolved. Cool slightly. In a
blender or food processor, purée together the
gelatine, cottage cheese, soft cheese, sugar,
cream and lemon rind until smooth.

Pour mixture into a bowl and gently stir in
strawberries until evenly mixed. Pour
mixture over crumb base and chill in the
refrigerator until set. When set, cut into
squares and decorate each square with kiwi
fruit slices.

Makes 12.

Cals/Kj per square: 172/726   Fat per square: 8.6 g

——————MANDARIN DELIGHT——————

300 g (10 oz) can mandarin segments in fruit juice
12.5 g (½ oz) packet sugar-free mandarin or tangerine
    jelly crystals
about 300 ml (10 fl oz/1¼ cups) unsweetened
    apple juice
150 ml (5 fl oz/²⁄₃ cup) Greek yogurt
25 g (1 oz/¼ cup) toasted flaked almonds
orange rind, to decorate

Drain mandarins over a bowl, reserving the juice.

Dissolve jelly crystals in 300 ml (10 fl oz/ 1¼ cups) boiling water, then make up liquid to 550 ml (20 fl oz/2½ cups) with reserved mandarin juice and apple juice. Leave aside until just beginning to set. Stir mandarins into the jelly and pour into individual glass serving dishes. Chill in the refrigerator until set.

Top each dessert with Greek yogurt and decorate with flaked almonds and orange rind before serving.

Serves 4.

Total Cals/Kj: 572/2194   Total fat: 25.4 g
Cals/Kj per portion: 143/549   Fat per portion: 6.3 g

Note: Instead of mixing the mandarins into the jelly, put mandarins in base of dishes and pour jelly over. Leave to set, then top with yogurt.

———LEMON PUDDING———

55 g (2 oz/¼ cup) low fat spread
115 g (4 oz/½ cup) caster sugar
grated rind and juice of 1 lemon
2 eggs, separated
55 g (2 oz/½ cup) self-raising flour
300 ml (10 fl oz/1¼ cups) skimmed milk
grated lemon rind, to decorate

Preheat oven to 200C (400F/Gas 6). In a
bowl, beat together low fat spread, sugar and
lemon rind until light and fluffy.

Add egg yolks and mix well. Sift flour into
mixture and fold in using a metal spoon. Add
lemon juice and milk and mix thoroughly. In
a separate bowl, whisk egg whites until stiff
and then fold them carefully into lemon
mixture, using a metal spoon.

Pour mixture into a greased 850 ml (30 fl oz/
3¾ cup) ovenproof dish. Stand dish in a
shallow tin of water. Bake in oven for 45
minutes until top is spongy to touch and
golden brown. Serve immediately decorated
with lemon rind.

Serves 6.

Total Cals/Kj: 1177/4956   Total fat: 39.4 g
Cals/Kj per portion: 196/826   Fat per portion: 6.5 g

—PEACH SOUFFLÉ OMELETTE—

1 peach
6 teaspoons reduced sugar peach or apricot jam, warmed
2 eggs, separated
1 teaspoon caster sugar
2 teaspoons icing sugar

Peel, stone and chop peach roughly. In a small bowl, mix together peach and warmed jam. Set aside. In a bowl, whisk egg yolks and sugar together until creamy. In a separate bowl, whisk egg whites until stiff.

Heat a 17.5 cm (7 in) non-stick omelette pan over a medium heat for a couple of minutes. Fold egg whites into egg yolk mixture and pour into the pan. Cook over a moderate heat for 2-3 minutes, until omelette is golden brown on the underside. Place pan under a preheated moderate grill for a few more minutes, until top is golden brown. Place omelette on a warm serving plate.

Spread with peach and jam mixture and fold omelette over. Sift icing sugar over top of omelette and, using a metal skewer, mark a criss-cross pattern in the sugar. Serve immediately, cut in half.

Serves 2.

Total Cals/Kj: 369/1546   Total fat: 16.3 g
Cals/Kj per portion: 185/773   Fat per portion: 8.1 g

ROSY DESSERT PEARS

4 large Conference pears
425 ml (15 fl oz/1¾ cups) red wine
150 ml (5 fl oz/⅔ cup) unsweetened orange juice
85 g (3 oz/½ cup) soft brown sugar
grated orange rind, to decorate

Preheat oven to 200C (400F/Gas 6). Carefully peel pears, leaving stalks intact and the fruits whole. Place in an ovenproof dish.

In a measuring jug, mix together red wine, orange juice and sugar. Pour the liquid over the pears. (The pears may need to be laid on their sides.) Cover dish and bake in oven for 1 hour until pears are softened.

Carefully lift pears out of dish and place upright on a serving dish or individual dishes. Pour liquid into a saucepan and boil rapidly until it is reduced. Spoon some of the liquid over the pears. Decorate with orange rind. Serve hot with reduced fat cream or Greek yogurt, if wished.

Serves 4.

Total Cals/Kj: 966/4105   Total fat: 0.9 g
Cals/Kj per portion: 242/1026   Fat per portion: 0.2 g

—GOOSEBERRY BROWN BETTY—

450 g (1lb) gooseberries
85 g (3 oz/¾ cup) plain flour
pinch of salt
1 teaspoon ground cinnamon
85 g (3 oz/1 cup) rolled oats
55 g (2 oz/⅓ cup) soft brown sugar
55 g (2 oz/¼ cup) low fat spread
6 teaspoons clear honey

Preheat oven to 180C (350F/Gas 4). Place gooseberries in a saucepan with 2 tablespoons water. Cover and cook gently until fruit is just soft.

Sift flour, salt and cinnamon into a bowl. Stir in oats and sugar and mix well. Rub in low fat spread until evenly mixed. Place half the gooseberries in a 1.2 litre (40 fl oz/5 cup) ovenproof dish, dribble over half the honey and top with half the oat mixture.

Repeat these layers once more, finishing with a layer of oat mixture. Bake in oven for 30-40 minutes until topping is crisp and golden brown. Serve hot with low fat yogurt or custard.

Serves 6.

Total Cals/Kj: 1309/5509   Total fat: 30.8 g
Cals/Kj per portion: 218/918   Fat per portion: 5.1 g

——— PLUM BATTER PUDDING ———

115 g (4 oz/1 cup) plain flour
pinch of salt
1 egg, beaten
300 ml (10 fl oz/1¼ cups) skimmed milk
1 tablespoon sunflower oil
9 red dessert plums
55 g (2 oz/¼ cup) caster sugar

Preheat oven to 220C (425F/Gas 7). To make batter, sift flour and salt into bowl, make a well in the centre and add beaten egg.

Gradually beat in milk until mixture is smooth. Grease a 6-hole muffin or deep bun tin and heat in the oven for 2-3 minutes. Halve and stone plums.

Remove muffin or bun tin from oven and quickly arrange plums in base of each. Sprinkle with sugar. Pour batter over fruit. Bake in oven for 20-25 minutes until risen and brown. Serve immediately.

Serves 6.

Total Cals/Kj: 1092/4605   Total fat: 25.0 g
Cals/Kj per portion: 182/768   Fat per portion: 4.1 g

Variation: Use apricots or damsons in place of plums.

──── PEAR & DATE SLICES ────

450 g (1 lb) pears
85 g (3 oz/⅓ cup) caster sugar
1 teaspoon ground cinnamon
115 g (4 oz/⅔ cup) dried dates, chopped
12 sheets filo pastry
55 g (2 oz/¼ cup) low fat spread, melted
6 teaspoons clear honey, warmed

Preheat oven to 150C (300F/Gas 2). Peel, core and slice pears. Place in a saucepan with 2 tablespoons water. Cover and cook over a low heat until just softened. Add sugar, cinnamon and dates, mix well and cool slightly. Trim filo pastry sheets into sheets measuring 27.5 × 17.5 cm (11 × 7 in).

Place one sheet of pastry in the base of a 27.5 × 17.5 cm (11 × 7 in) baking tin. Brush lightly with melted fat. Place another sheet of pastry on top, brush lightly with melted fat and repeat with another 2 sheets pastry. Place half the fruit mixture on top. Place 4 sheets of pastry on top of fruit, brushing each sheet lightly with melted fat.

Repeat with remaining fruit mixture and pastry sheets, brushing each sheet with melted fat. Cut through the layers to make 12 slices. Bake in oven for 1-1½ hours until golden brown on top. Spoon warm honey evenly over the slices. Allow to stand for 5 minutes, then serve with low fat custard or cream.

Makes 12.

Cals/Kj per slice: 147/621   Fat per slice: 2.5 g

– ORANGE SEMOLINA PUDDING –

550 ml (20 fl oz/2½ cups) skimmed milk
15 g (½ oz/3 teaspoons) low fat spread
45 g (1½ oz/¼ cup) wholewheat semolina
55 g (2 oz/¼ cup) caster sugar
grated rind of 1 orange
grated orange rind, to decorate

Preheat oven to 200C (400F/Gas 6). In a saucepan, heat together milk and low fat spread until almost boiling. Sprinkle on semolina.

Bring to the boil and cook for a further 3 minutes, stirring continuously. Remove from heat and stir in sugar and orange rind, mixing well.

Pour mixture into a greased 850 ml (30 fl oz/ 3¾ cup) ovenproof dish. Bake in oven for 30 minutes until lightly browned. Serve immediately, decorated with orange rind and accompanied by fresh fruit, if wished.

Serves 4.

Total Cals/Kj: 616/2605   Total fat: 7.3 g
Cals/Kj per portion: 154/651   Fat per portion: 1.8 g

── HOT LEMON SOUFFLÉ ──

45 g (1½ oz/9 teaspoons) low fat spread
45 g (1½ oz/6 tablespoons) plain flour
225 ml (8 fl oz/1 cup) skimmed milk
grated rind and juice of 1 lemon
4 eggs, separated
55 g (2 oz/¼ cup) caster sugar
1 tablespoon icing sugar

Preheat oven to 180C (350F/Gas 4). Grease a
1.25 litre (40 fl oz/5 cup) soufflé dish. In a
saucepan, melt low fat spread, stir in flour
and cook slowly for 2 minutes, stirring
continuously.

Gradually add milk and beat until smooth.
Cook gently for 2 minutes. Beat lemon rind
and juice into sauce, together with egg yolks.
Beat in sugar, mixing well. In a separate
bowl, whisk egg whites until stiff. Using a
metal spoon, gently fold egg whites into
lemon mixture.

Spoon lemon mixture into soufflé dish. Bake
in oven for 45 minutes until well risen and
golden brown. Dust with sifted icing sugar
and serve immediately.

Serves 6.

Total Cals/Kj: 1124/4708   Total fat: 51.1 g
Cals/Kj per portion: 187/785   Fat per portion: 8.5 g

- APRICOT & ORANGE COMPOTE -

55 g (2 oz/⅓ cup) soft brown sugar
1 teaspoon ground cinnamon
1 teaspoon ground nutmeg
1 teaspoon ground cloves
2 tablespoons unsweetened orange juice
1 tablespoon Cointreau or orange liqueur
400 g (14 oz) can apricot halves in fruit juice
2 large oranges, peeled and thickly sliced

Place 550 ml (20 fl oz/2½ cups) water in a saucepan and stir in sugar. Dissolve sugar over a low heat, stirring occasionally.

Add all the spices and orange juice to pan. Bring to the boil, reduce the heat and simmer for 15 minutes.

Add the Cointreau, apricots and juice and oranges and stir gently to mix. Simmer gently for a further 10-15 minutes. Serve immediately with reduced fat cream or Greek yogurt sprinkled with cinnamon.

Serves 4.

Total Cals/Kj: 550/2357	Total fat: 3.9 g
Cals/Kj per portion: 138/589	Fat per portion: 0.9 g

Note: This dessert is also delicious served chilled with Greek yogurt.

SPICY CARROT RING

115 g (4 oz/½ cup) low fat spread
115 g (4 oz/⅔ cup) soft brown sugar
2 eggs, beaten
175 g (6 oz/1½ cups) self-raising flour
2 teaspoons ground mixed spice
grated rind and juice of 1 lemon
55 g (2 oz/⅓ cup) raisins
225 g (8 oz) carrots, peeled and coarsely grated
1 tablespoon icing sugar

Preheat oven to 180C (350F/Gas 4). In a
bowl, cream together low fat spread and sugar
until light and fluffy.

Gradually add beaten eggs, beating well after
each addition, then fold in flour and mixed
spice. Add lemon rind and juice, raisins and
carrots. Stir gently but thoroughly to mix.

Spoon mixture into a greased 1.2 litre
(40 fl oz/5 cup) ring mould. Bake in oven for
30-40 minutes until golden brown. Turn out
onto a wire rack and dust with sifted icing
sugar. Serve immediately in slices, with low
fat custard.

Serves 8.

Total Cals/Kj: 2011/8456   Total fat: 65.6 g
Cals/Kj per portion: 251/1057   Fat per portion: 8.2 g

—— HARVEST CRUNCHIES ——

225 g (8 oz) cooking apples
225 g (8 oz) pears
115 g (4 oz) blackberries
2 tablespoons unsweetened orange juice
55 g (2 oz/⅓ cup) soft brown sugar
25 g (1 oz/6 teaspoons) low fat spread
2 tablespoons clear honey
55 g (2 oz/⅔ cup) rolled oats
55 g (2 oz/2 cups) bran flakes
mint leaves, to decorate

Preheat oven to 180C (350F/Gas 4). Peel,
core and slice apples and pears. Place in a
saucepan with the blackberries and orange
juice.

Cover and cook gently until just softened.
Add sugar and mix well. In a separate saucepan, melt low fat spread and honey over a low
heat. Stir in oats and bran flakes and mix
well. Place fruit mixture in the bases of 6
small ovenproof dishes.

Spoon crunch mixture over fruit. Bake in
oven for 25-30 minutes until crisp and brown
on top. Decorate with mint leaves and serve
immediately with low fat custard or reduced
fat cream, if wished.

Serves 6.

Total Cals/Kj: 962/4061   Total fat: 15.6 g
Cals/Kj per portion: 160/677   Fat per portion: 2.6 g

Variation: Replace the bran flakes with a
crunchy cereal of your own choice.

-MANGO & LYCHEE TURNOVERS-

3 teaspoons cornflour
3 teaspoons sugar
3 tablespoons unsweetened orange juice
1 teaspoon lemon juice
1 teaspoon ground nutmeg
1 mango
10 lychees
8 sheets filo pastry
55 g (2 oz/¼ cup) low fat spread, melted
1 tablespoon icing sugar

Preheat oven to 200C (400F/Gas 6). In a saucepan, blend cornflour and sugar with 3 tablespoons water. Add orange juice, lemon juice and nutmeg and mix well.

Heat gently over a low heat until mixture thickens, stirring all the time. Simmer sauce for 3 minutes, then allow to cool. Peel, stone and roughly chop mango and lychees. Add fruit to cooled sauce, mixing well. To make each turnover, cut each filo sheet in half crosswise to make two 10 cm (4 in) squares (total of 16 squares). Brush 2 squares of pastry lightly with melted fat and place one on top of the other. Place some filling in the centre of the pastry, fold diagonally in half and press edges to seal.

Place on a greased baking sheet and brush lightly with melted fat. Repeat with remaining pastry squares and filling to make 8 turnovers. Bake in oven for 30 minutes, until golden brown and crisp. Dust with sifted icing sugar and serve immediately with low fat ice cream.

Makes 8.

Cals/Kj per turnover: 127/535   Fat per turnover: 3.6 g

EVE'S PUDDING

350 g (12 oz) cooking apples
55 g (2 oz/⅓ cup) soft brown sugar
55 g (2 oz/¼ cup) low fat spread
55 g (2 oz/¼ cup) caster sugar
1 egg, beaten
115 g (4 oz/1 cup) self-raising flour
2 tablespoons skimmed milk
25 g (1 oz/¼ cup) flaked almonds

Preheat oven to 180C (350F/Gas 4). Peel, core and slice apples and place in the base of a greased 850 ml (30 fl oz/3¾ cup) ovenproof dish.

Sprinkle over brown sugar. In a bowl, cream together low fat spread and caster sugar until light and fluffy. Gradually add beaten egg, beating well after each addition, then fold in flour. Stir in milk, mixing gently but thoroughly.

Spread mixture over apples and sprinkle almonds on top. Bake in oven for 30-40 minutes until apples are tender and sponge is golden brown. Serve with Greek yogurt or a sprinkling of icing sugar, if wished.

Serves 6.

Total Cals/Kj: 1408/5916   Total fat: 45.8 g
Cals/Kj per portion: 235/986   Fat per portion: 7.6 g

BAKED BANANAS

4 medium bananas
2 tablespoons brandy
6 tablespoons unsweetened orange juice
25 g (1 oz/2 tablespoons) soft brown sugar
150 ml (5 fl oz/⅔ cup) reduced fat single (light) cream
orange twists, to decorate

Preheat oven to 180C (350F/Gas 4). Peel bananas and slice diagonally.

Place banana slices in an ovenproof dish. In a bowl, mix brandy, orange juice and sugar together and pour the mixture over the bananas. Cover dish and bake in oven for 30 minutes.

Place bananas into a serving dish or individual dishes, then pour juice and cream over. Decorate with orange twists. Serve with low fat yogurt decorated with orange rind.

Serves 4.

Total Cals/Kj: 802/3404   Total fat: 15.5 g
Cals/Kj per portion: 201/851   Fat per portion: 3.8 g

—CAROB & CHERRY SPONGE—

400 g (14 oz) can cherries in fruit juice
100 g (3½ oz/7 tablespoons) low fat spread
100 g (3½ oz/½ cup) caster sugar
2 eggs, beaten
175 g (6 oz/1½ cups) self-raising flour, sifted
9 teaspoons carob flour, sifted
3 tablespoons skimmed milk

Place cherries and a little juice in the base of a greased 1.25 litre (40 fl oz/5 cup) pudding basin. In a bowl, cream together low fat spread and sugar until light and fluffy.

Gradually add beaten eggs, beating well after each addition. Using a metal spoon, fold in sifted flour and carob flour, then add milk and mix gently to combine. Place pudding mixture on top of cherries and level the surface. Cover with a double layer of greased greaseproof paper and secure with string.

Place in a saucepan of gently boiling water to come half way up sides of basin and steam for 1½ hours. To serve, turn out carefully onto a plate and serve with low fat custard.

Serves 8.

Total Cals/Kj: 1985/8363   Total fat: 58.7 g
Cals/Kj per portion: 248/1045   Fat per portion: 7.3 g

APRICOT PUDDING

400 g (4 oz) can apricot halves in fruit juice
6 glace cherries
100 g (3½ oz/7 tablespoons) low fat spread
100 g (3½ oz/½ cup) soft brown sugar
2 eggs, beaten
225 g (8 oz/2 cups) self-raising flour
5 tablespoons skimmed milk

Preheat oven to 180C (350F/Gas 4). Drain apricots and halve cherries. Place cherries, cut side down, over the base of a greased 1.5 litre (50 fl oz/6⅔ cup) ovenproof dish and place apricot halves on top.

In a bowl, cream together low fat spread and sugar until light and fluffy. Gradually add beaten eggs, beating well after each addition. Fold in flour and milk to give a soft dropping consistency.

Spread mixture over apricots. Bake in oven for 45 minutes until well risen and golden brown. Turn out onto a warmed serving dish and serve with low fat ice cream.

Serves 8.

Total Cals/Kj: 2000/8427   Total fat: 59.3 g
Cals/Kj per portion: 250/1053   Fat per portion: 7.4 g

RHUBARB & APPLE CHARLOTTE

575 g (1¼ lb) can rhubarb in fruit juice
225 g (8 oz) cooking apples
55 g (2 oz/⅓ cup) soft brown sugar
55 g (2 oz/¼ cup) low fat spread
175 g (6 oz/3 cups) fresh wholemeal breadcrumbs
300 ml (10 fl oz/1¼ cups) unsweetened orange juice

Preheat oven to 190C (375F/Gas 5). Drain the rhubarb and peel, core and slice the apples.

Place half the rhubarb in the base of a 1.5 litre (50 fl oz/6⅔ cup) ovenproof dish. Cover with half the apple slices. Sprinkle over half the sugar and dot with some low fat spread. Cover with half the breadcrumbs. Repeat the layers, ending with a layer of breadcrumbs.

Pour orange juice over the pudding. Bake in oven for 40 minutes. Serve with reduced fat cream.

Serves 6.

Total Cals/Kj: 1259/5334   Total fat: 26.6 g
Cals/Kj per portion: 210/889   Fat per portion: 4.4 g

Variation: Use fresh white, brown or Granary breadcrumbs in place of wholemeal breadcrumbs.

— BLACKBERRY APPLE COBBLER —

450 g (1lb) cooking apples
225 g (8 oz) blackberries
85 g (3 oz/⅓ cup) caster sugar
225 g (8 oz/2 cups) self-raising flour
pinch of salt
2 teaspoons ground mixed spice
45 g (1½ oz/9 teaspoons) low fat spread
about 150 ml (5 fl oz/⅔ cup) skimmed milk

Preheat oven to 220C (425F/Gas 7). Peel, core and slice apples and place in a saucepan with blackberries and 2 tablespoons water. Cover pan and cook gently until just soft. Add 55 g (2 oz/¼ cup) sugar and put in a 1.5 litre (50 fl oz/6⅔ cup) ovenproof dish.

Sift flour into a bowl with salt and mixed spice. Rub in low fat spread until mixture resembles breadcrumbs, then stir in remaining sugar. Add enough milk to bind dough. Roll out dough on a lightly floured surface and cut out twelve 5 cm (2 in) scones.

Place scones around edge of dish on top of fruit, overlapping them slightly. Brush scones with a little milk. Bake in oven for 15-20 minutes until scones are well risen and brown. Serve with low fat custard.

Serves 6.

Total Cals/Kj: 1503/6348   Total fat: 21.6 g
Cals/Kj per portion: 251/1058   Fat per portion: 3.6 g

——— RUM & RAISIN CRÊPES ———

CRÊPES:
55 g (2 oz/½ cup) wholemeal plain flour
55 g (2 oz/½ cup) plain flour
pinch of salt
1 egg
300 ml (10 fl oz/1¼ cups) skimmed milk
2 teaspoons sunflower oil
SAUCE:
3 teaspoons cornflour
55 g (2 oz/⅓ cup) soft brown sugar
300 ml (10 fl oz/1¼ cups) unsweetened orange juice
55 g (2 oz/⅓ cup) raisins
3 tablespoons rum

Sift flours and salt into a large bowl and make a well in the centre.

Beat together egg and milk and pour into the well. Using a wooden spoon, gradually mix flour into liquid, keeping batter smooth. Beat well. Leave to stand. Meanwhile, make sauce. In a saucepan, blend cornflour and sugar with orange juice. Stir in raisins. Heat gently, stirring continuously until sauce thickens. Add rum and simmer for 3 minutes. Keep warm while making crêpes. Heat a 17.5 cm (7 in) heavy-based frying pan and grease lightly with oil.

Pour in just enough batter to cover the bottom of the pan. Cook over a medium heat for 1-2 minutes, until underside is lightly browned. Turn or toss crêpe and cook other side for the same amount of time. Turn out and keep warm while cooking remaining crêpes. Serve crêpes with rum and raisin sauce poured over.

Makes 8.

Cals/Kj per crêpe: 161/679   Fat per crêpe: 2.6 g

–RASPBERRY & APPLE STRUDEL–

225 g (8 oz) cooking apples
225 g (8 oz) raspberries
55 g (2 oz/¼ cup) caster sugar
55 g (2 oz/½ cup) chopped mixed nuts
1 teaspoon ground cinnamon
8 sheets filo pastry
55 g (2 oz/¼ cup) low fat spread
1 tablespoon icing sugar

Preheat oven to 190C (375F/Gas 5). Peel, core and slice apples. Place in a saucepan with raspberries and 2 tablespoons water. Cover and cook gently until just soft. Stir in sugar and cool. Add nuts and cinnamon and mix well.

Place one sheet of pastry on a sheet of baking parchment and brush lightly with melted fat. Place another sheet of pastry on top and layer all 8 sheets of pastry on top of one another, brushing each one lightly with melted fat. Spoon fruit mixture over pastry leaving a 2.5 cm (1 in) border uncovered all around edge. Fold these edges over fruit mixture.

With a long side towards you, using baking parchment, roll up strudel. Carefully place it on a greased baking sheet, seam-side down. Brush it lightly with melted fat. Bake in oven for about 40 minutes until golden brown. Dust with sifted icing sugar.

Serves 8.

Total Cals/Kj: 1409/5902   Total fat: 57.5 g
Cals/Kj per portion: 176/738   Fat per portion: 7.1 g

-SULTANA & CARROT PUDDING-

115 g (4 oz/½ cup) low fat spread
85 g (3 oz/½ cup) soft brown sugar
2 eggs, beaten
175 g (6 oz/1½ cups) self-raising flour, sifted
115 g (4 oz) carrots, peeled and coarsely grated
55 g (2 oz/⅓ cup) sultanas
3 tablespoons skimmed milk

In a bowl, cream together low fat spread and sugar until light and fluffy. Gradually add beaten eggs, beating well after each addition.

Using a metal spoon, fold in sifted flour, carrots, sultanas and milk, mixing gently to combine. Place mixture in a greased 1.25 litre (40 fl oz/5 cup) pudding basin and level the surface.

Cover with a double layer of greased grease-proof paper and secure with string. Place in a saucepan of gently boiling water to come halfway up sides of basin. Steam for 1½ hours. To serve, turn out carefully onto a plate and serve with low fat custard or reduced fat cream.

Serves 8.

Total Cals/Kj: 1810/7605   Total fat: 65.0 g
Cals/Kj per portion: 226/951   Fat per portion: 8.1 g

BREAD PUDDING

6 thin slices wholemeal bread, crusts removed
25 g (1 oz/6 teaspoons) low fat spread
2 tablespoons reduced sugar strawberry jam
55 g (2 oz/⅓ cup) sultanas
25 g (1 oz/6 teaspoons) soft brown sugar
2 eggs
550 ml (20 fl oz/2½ cups) skimmed milk

Spread one side of the bread slices with low fat spread. Spread the other side with jam.

Cut into small triangles or fingers. Place half in a greased 1.25 litre (40 fl oz/5 cup) oven-proof dish, sprinkle with sultanas and half the sugar. Top with remaining bread, low fat spread side up and sprinkle with remaining sugar.

In a bowl, whisk together eggs and milk and strain this mixture into dish over bread. Leave to stand for 30 minutes, so that the bread absorbs some of the liquid. Meanwhile, preheat oven to 160C (325F/Gas 3). Bake in oven for about 1 hour until set and golden brown. Serve immediately with low fat yogurt sprinkled with cinnamon.

Serves 6.

Total Cals/Kj: 1112/5186   Total fat: 30.6 g
Cals/Kj per portion: 185/864   Fat per portion: 5.1 g

──STRAWBERRY YOGURT ICE──

450 g (1 lb) strawberries
115 g (4 oz/½ cup) caster sugar
300 ml (10 fl oz/1¼ cups) low fat strawberry yogurt
225 g (8 oz/1 cup) skimmed milk soft cheese
mint sprigs and fresh strawberries, to decorate

Purée strawberries in a blender or food processor until smooth.

Add caster sugar, yogurt and soft cheese and blend until thoroughly mixed. Pour mixture into a chilled, shallow plastic container. Cover and freeze for 1½-2 hours or until mixture is mushy in consistency. Turn into a chilled bowl and beat with a fork or whisk until smooth.

Return mixture to container, cover and freeze until firm. Transfer to the refrigerator for 30 minutes before serving to soften. Serve in scoops, decorated with mint sprigs and fresh strawberries.

Serves 6.

Total Cals/Kj: 1013/4297   Total fat: 3.1 g
Cals/Kj per portion: 169/716   Fat per portion: 0.5 g

KIWI WATER ICE

6 kiwi fruit
1 tablespoon lemon juice
115 g (4 oz/½ cup) caster sugar
4 ripe passion fruit

Peel kiwi fruit and place in a blender or food processor with lemon juice. Blend until smooth and then set aside.

Place caster sugar in a saucepan with 300 ml (10 fl oz/1¼ cups) water. Bring slowly to the boil and boil gently for 10 minutes. Add kiwi purée, mix well and allow to cool. Put cooled mixture into a chilled, shallow plastic container. Cover and freeze for 1½-2 hours or until the mixture is mushy in consistency. Turn into a chilled bowl.

Cut each passion fruit in half and scoop out flesh. Add to kiwi water ice. Beat with a fork or whisk until smooth. Return mixture to container, cover and freeze until firm. Transfer to the refrigerator for about 15 minutes before serving to soften. Serve in individual dishes, accompanied by sweet biscuits.

Serves 6.

Total Cals/Kj: 681/2888   Total fat: 2.1 g
Cals/Kj per portion: 114/481   Fat per portion: 0.3 g

COFFEE BOMBE

350 ml (12 fl oz/1½ cups) reduced fat single
  (light) cream
150 ml (5 fl oz/⅔ cup) reduced fat double
  (heavy) cream
4 tablespoons Greek yogurt
2 teaspoons instant coffee powder
55 g (2 oz/⅓ cup) icing sugar, sifted

In a large bowl, mix creams and yogurt together.

Dissolve coffee powder in 1 tablespoon warm water. Fold into cream mixture with the icing sugar and mix gently but thoroughly. Pour mixture into a lightly greased 850 ml (30 fl oz/ 3¾ cup) bombe mould or pudding basin. Freeze until firm.

Transfer bombe to the refrigerator 45 minutes before serving to soften slightly. Turn out onto a serving dish.

Serves 8.

Total Cals/Kj: 1071/4462   Total fat: 73.7 g
Cals/Kj per portion: 134/558   Fat per portion: 9.2 g

Variation: Decorate with flaked almonds, if wished, but this will increase the calorie and fat count.

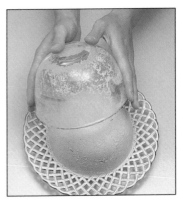

MIXED BERRY SHERBET

115 g (4 oz) raspberries
115 g (4 oz) blackcurrants
115 g (4 oz) strawberries
115 g (4 oz/½ cup) caster sugar
550 ml (20 fl oz/2½ cups) skimmed milk
150 ml (5 fl oz/⅔ cup) reduced fat double
   (heavy) cream
150 ml (5 fl oz/⅔ cup) reduced fat
   (single) cream
fresh berries, to decorate

Place fruit and sugar in a saucepan with 2 tablespoons water. Cover and cook gently until soft. Allow to cool completely.

Place cooked fruit, milk and creams into a blender or food processor and blend until smooth. Pour mixture into a chilled, shallow plastic container. Cover and freeze for 1½-2 hours or until the mixture is mushy in consistency.

Turn into a chilled bowl and beat with a fork or whisk until smooth. Return mixture to container, cover and freeze until firm. Transfer to the refrigerator for 30 minutes before serving to soften. Serve in scoops, decorated with mixed berries.

Serves 6.

Total Cals/Kj: 1274/5355   Total fat: 51.1 g
Cals/Kj per portion: 212/893   Fat per portion: 8.5 g

MANDARIN CRUSH

300 g (10 oz) can mandarins in fruit juice
55 g (2 oz/¼ cup) caster sugar
425 ml (15 fl oz/1¾ cups) Greek yogurt
fresh orange wedges and rind, to decorate

Place mandarins and juice, sugar and Greek yogurt in a blender or food processor and blend until smooth and well mixed.

Pour mandarin and yogurt mixture into a chilled, shallow plastic container. Cover and freeze for 1½-2 hours or until the mixture is mushy in consistency. Turn into a chilled bowl and beat with a fork or whisk until the mixture is smooth.

Return mixture to container, cover and freeze until firm. Transfer to the refrigerator for 30 minutes before serving to soften. Serve in scoops, decorated with orange wedges and rind.

Serves 4.

Total Cals/Kj: 764/3208   Total fat: 31.9 g
Cals/Kj per portion: 191/802   Fat per portion: 7.9 g

— CAROB RAISIN ICE CREAM —

450 ml (16 fl oz/2 cups) skimmed milk
3 tablespoons sugar
3 teaspoons cornflour
pinch of salt
3 egg yolks
115 g (4 oz) plain (dark) carob drops
115 g (4 oz/⅔ cup) raisins
115 g (4 oz/½ cup) low fat soft cheese

Put milk into a saucepan and heat gently until almost boiling. In a bowl, blend sugar, cornflour, salt and egg yolks together, then gradually pour on milk, stirring all the time.

Pour mixture back into saucepan and heat gently until mixture thickens, stirring continuously. Bring to the boil and boil for 1 minute. Melt carob drops in a small bowl set over a pan of simmering water. Add melted carob and raisins to custard, mixing well. Allow mixture to cool. Gradually blend soft cheese into custard, mixing well. Pour mixture into a chilled, shallow plastic container. Cover and freeze for 1½-2 hours or until the mixture is mushy in consistency. Turn into a chilled bowl and beat with a fork or whisk until smooth.

Return mixture to container, cover and freeze for 1 hour. Beat mixture as before and return to container. Cover and freeze until firm. Transfer to the refrigerator for 30 minutes before serving to soften. Serve in individual glass dishes or glasses, accompanied by sweet biscuits, if wished.

Serves 6.

Total Cals/Kj: 1257/5295   Total fat: 27.8 g
Cals/Kj per portion: 209/883   Fat per portion: 4.6 g

PLUM ICE

300 g (10 oz) plums or damsons
55 g (2 oz/¼ cup) caster sugar
300 ml (10 fl oz/1¼ cups) reduced fat evaporated milk
300 ml (10 fl oz/1¼ cups) reduced fat single
   (light) cream
mint sprigs, to decorate

Place plums or damsons in a saucepan with sugar and 2 tablespoons water. Cover and cook gently until just soft. Allow to cool, then remove stones. Place plums or damsons in a blender or food processor and blend until smooth. Allow to cool completely.

In a large bowl, whisk evaporated milk until thick. Fold in cream and plum or damson purée, mixing gently but thoroughly. Pour mixture into a chilled, shallow plastic container. Cover and freeze for 1½-2 hours or until the mixture is mushy in consistency. Turn into a chilled bowl and beat with a fork or whisk until smooth.

Return mixture to container, cover and freeze for 1 hour. Beat mixture as before and return to container. Cover and freeze until firm. Transfer to the refrigerator for 30 minutes before serving to soften. Serve in scoops, decorated with fresh mint sprigs.

Serves 6.

Total Cals/Kj: 1009/4251   Total fat: 40.5 g
Cals/Kj per portion: 168/709   Fat per portion: 6.7 g

—BROWN BREAD ICE CREAM—

150 g (5 oz/2½ cups) fresh wholemeal breadcrumbs
55 g (2 oz/⅓ cup) soft brown sugar
425 ml (15 fl oz/1¾ cups) low fat ready-made
    cold custard
150 ml (5 fl oz/⅔ cup) Greek yogurt
grated rind and juice of 1 lemon
25 g (1 oz/2 tablespoons) icing sugar, sifted
lemon rind, to decorate

Preheat oven to 200C (400F/Gas 6). Place breadcrumbs on a greased baking sheet and sprinkle sugar over the top. Bake in oven for 10 minutes, stirring occasionally, until sugar caramelizes and crumbs are golden.

Cool crumbs and break up roughly with a fork. In a bowl, mix together custard, yogurt, lemon rind and juice and icing sugar. Pour into a chilled, shallow plastic container. Cover and freeze for 1½-2 hours or until mixture is mushy in consistency.

Turn into a chilled bowl and beat with a fork or whisk until smooth. Fold in breadcrumbs. Return mixture to container, cover and freeze until firm. Transfer to the refrigerator for 45 minutes before serving to soften. Serve in scoops, decorated with lemon rind and accompanied by wafer biscuits.

Serves 6.

Total Cals/Kj: 1374/5816   Total fat: 19.9 g
Cals/Kj per portion: 229/969   Fat per portion: 3.3 g

BLACKCURRANT ICED TERRINE

450 ml (16 fl oz/2 cups) skimmed milk
4-5 tablespoons granulated sugar
3 teaspoons cornflour
pinch of salt
3 egg yolks
150 ml (5 fl oz/²⁄₃ cup) reduced fat double
  (heavy) cream
250 ml (9 fl oz/1 cup) reduced fat single
  (light) cream
1 teaspoon vanilla essence
225 g (8 oz) blackcurrants
85 g (3 oz/½ cup) icing sugar, sifted
mint sprigs, to decorate

Put milk in a saucepan and heat gently until almost boiling.

In a bowl, blend granulated sugar, cornflour, salt and egg yolk. Gradually pour on milk, whisking. Pour back into pan. Heat until thick, stirring. Bring to the boil and boil for 1 minute. Pour into a bowl and leave to cool. In a bowl, mix creams together and carefully fold into custard with vanilla essence. Pour mixture into a 1 kg (2 lb) loaf tin and freeze for 1½-2 hours until mushy. Turn into a bowl and beat with a fork until smooth. Return to loaf tin and freeze until firm. Put blackcurrants in a pan with 2 tablespoons water. Cover and cook until soft; cool.

In a blender or food processor, blend blackcurrants and icing sugar together until smooth. The sauce may be sieved at this stage to remove pips, if wished. To serve terrine, transfer to the refrigerator for 30 minutes before serving to soften. Turn terrine out onto a serving plate and pour blackcurrant sauce over the top. Decorate with mint.

Serves 8.

Total Cals/Kj: 1767/7423   Total fat: 78.5 g
Cals/Kj per portion: 221/928   Fat per portion: 9.8 g

—LEMON & LIME YOGURT ICE—

550 ml (20 fl oz/2½ cups) low fat plain yogurt
85 g (3 oz/⅓ cup) caster sugar
grated rind and juice of 1 lemon
grated rind and juice of 1 lime
lime slices and strips of lemon and lime rind, to decorate

In a bowl, beat yogurt and sugar together until sugar has dissolved.

Add grated fruit rinds and juices and mix well. Pour into a chilled, shallow plastic container. Cover and freeze for 1½-2 hours or until mushy in consistency. Turn into a chilled bowl and beat with a fork or whisk until smooth. Return mixture to container, cover and freeze until firm.

Transfer to the refrigerator for 30 minutes before serving to soften. Serve in scoops, decorated with lime slices and strips of lime and lemon rind.

Serves 4.

Total Cals/Kj: 645/2736   Total fat: 4.4 g
Cals/Kj per portion: 161/684   Fat per portion: 1.1 g

Variation: For a slightly less tangy flavour, use the grated rind and juice of 1 orange in place of lime.

— BANANA & RUM ICE CREAM —

450 g (1 lb) bananas
300 ml (10 fl oz/1¼ cups) reduced fat single
   (light) cream
300 ml (10 fl oz/1¼ cups) low fat plain yogurt
9 teaspoons rum
5 tablespoons clear honey
25 g (1 oz/¼ cup) walnuts, chopped

Peel bananas, place in a large bowl and mash with a fork.

Add cream, yogurt, rum, honey and walnuts and beat well to mix. Pour mixture into a chilled, shallow plastic container. Cover and freeze for 1½-2 hours or until the mixture is mushy in consistency. Turn into a chilled bowl and beat with a fork or whisk until smooth.

Return mixture to container, cover and freeze until firm. Transfer to the refrigerator 30 minutes before serving to soften. Serve in scoops in individual glasses with sweet biscuits.

Serves 6.

Total Cals/Kj: 1300/5472   Total fat: 48.8 g
Cals/Kj per portion: 216/912   Fat per portion: 8.1 g

FRESH FRUIT SAVARIN

25 g (1 oz) fresh yeast or 3 teaspoons dried yeast plus
   1 teaspoon sugar
6 tablespoons tepid skimmed milk
225 g (8 oz/2 cups) strong plain flour
½ teaspoon salt
6 teaspoons caster sugar
4 eggs, beaten
115 g (4 oz/½ cup) low fat spread
4 tablespoons clear honey
2 tablespoons brandy
350 g (12 oz) prepared fresh fruit, such as kiwi fruit,
   strawberries, peaches, raspberries, bananas
25 g (1 oz/¼ cup) flaked almonds, toasted
mint leaves, to decorate

Grease a 1.25 litre (40 fl oz/5 cup) savarin or ring mould. In a bowl, blend together yeast, milk and 55 g (2 oz/½ cup) flour. If using dried yeast, add the 1 teaspoon sugar and leave in a warm place until frothy (about 15 minutes). Add remaining flour to the yeast mixture, together with salt, sugar, eggs and low fat spread. Beat well for 5 minutes. Pour into mould, cover with a clean tea towel and leave to rise in a warm place for 15 minutes. Preheat oven to 200C (400F/Gas 6). Bake in oven for 30 minutes until golden brown.

Turn out savarin onto a plate. Place honey in a saucepan with 2 tablespoons water and heat gently until hot. Add brandy and spoon over savarin while still hot. Cool. Transfer to a serving plate and pile prepared fresh fruit into centre of savarin. Sprinkle with flaked almonds and decorate with mint leaves.

Serves 10.

Total Cals/Kj: 2326/9770   Total fat: 96.7 g
Cals/Kj per portion: 233/977   Fat per portion: 9.6 g

CRÈME CARAMELS

130 g (4½ oz/generous ½ cup) caster sugar
4 eggs
550 ml (20 fl oz/2½ cups) skimmed milk
few drops vanilla essence
slices of fruit and mint sprigs, to decorate (optional)

Preheat oven to 160C (325F/Gas 3). Put 115 g (4 oz/½ cup) sugar into a saucepan with 150 ml (5 fl oz/⅔ cup) water. Dissolve sugar slowly, then bring mixture to the boil and boil, without stirring, until it caramelizes to a golden brown colour.

Pour caramel into 6 warmed ramekin dishes, making sure the bottoms are completely covered. In a bowl, lightly whisk together eggs and remaining sugar. In a saucepan, warm milk and pour onto eggs and sugar. Whisk in vanilla essence, then strain over cooled caramels.

Stand ramekins in a shallow baking tin of water. Bake in oven for about 45 minutes until set. Leave in the dishes until cold, before turning out onto serving plates. Chill in the refrigerator until ready to serve. Decorate with slices of fruit and mint sprigs, if wished.

Serves 6.

Total Cals/Kj: 1135/4790   Total fat: 32.9 g
Cals/Kj per portion: 189/798   Fat per portion: 5.5 g

—HOT CHOCOLATE SOUFFLÉ—

85 g (3 oz) plain (dark) chocolate
150 ml (5 fl oz/²/₃ cup) skimmed milk
55 g (2 oz/¹/₄ cup) caster sugar
55 g (2 oz/¹/₂ cup) plain flour
15 g (¹/₂ oz/3 teaspoons) low fat spread
4 eggs, separated
1 tablespoon icing sugar

Preheat oven to 200C (400F/Gas 6). Grease a 1.25 litre (40 fl oz/5 cup) soufflé dish. Melt chocolate in a small bowl set over a pan of simmering water.

Place milk and sugar in a saucepan and heat gently until almost boiling. Add chocolate and mix well. In a bowl, blend flour with 2 tablespoons water. Gradually add chocolate mixture, blending well. Return to saucepan, bring gently to the boil, stirring continuously, and cook for 3 minutes. Add low fat spread in small pieces, mix well and leave to cool.

Stir in egg yolks. In a bowl, whisk egg whites until stiff. Using a metal spoon, fold egg whites into chocolate mixture. Pour into soufflé dish and bake in oven for about 35 minutes until well risen and firm to touch. Dust with sifted icing sugar and serve immediately.

Serves 6.

Total Cals/Kj: 1461/6128   Total fat: 64.0 g
Cals/Kj per portion: 244/1021   Fat per portion: 10.6 g

— PEACH MELBA CHEESECAKE —

55 g (2 oz/¼ cup) low fat spread
9 teaspoons clear honey
85 g (3 oz/3 cups) cornflakes
25 g (1 oz/¼ cup) chopped mixed nuts
400 g (14 oz) can peach slices in fruit juice
3 teaspoons powdered gelatine
175 g (6 oz) raspberries
300 g (10 oz/1 ¼ cups) low fat soft cheese
55 g (2 oz/¼ cup) caster sugar
150 ml (5 fl oz/⅔ cup) very low fat fromage frais
150 ml (5 fl oz/⅔ cup) reduced fat single
  (light) cream
fresh peach slices and raspberries, to decorate

In a saucepan, melt low fat spread and honey together over a low heat.

Stir in cornflakes and nuts, mixing well. Press mixture over base of a 20 cm (8 in) loose-bottomed tin and chill in the refrigerator. Drain peaches over a small bowl. Sprinkle gelatine over peach juice and leave for 2-3 minutes to soften. Stand bowl in a saucepan of hot water and stir until gelatine has dissolved. Cool slightly. Place peaches, raspberries, soft cheese, sugar, fromage frais, single (light) cream and gelatine in a blender or food processor and blend until smooth and well mixed.

Pour over chilled base and level surface. Chill in the refrigerator until set. To serve, remove cheesecake from tin and place on a serving plate. Decorate with fresh peach slices and raspberries and serve immediately.

Serves 8.

Total Cals/Kj: 1944/8174   Total fat: 57.5 g
Cals/Kj per portion: 243/1022   Fat per portion: 7.1 g

FESTIVAL GÂTEAU

3 egg whites
175 g (6 oz/¾ cup) caster sugar
½ teaspoon vanilla essence
½ teaspoon white wine vinegar
1 teaspoon cornflour
300 ml (10 fl oz/1¼ cups) reduced fat double
   (heavy) cream
2 kiwi fruit
115 g (4 oz) strawberries
115 g (4 oz) raspberries

Preheat oven to 110C (225F/Gas ¼). Draw two 20 cm (8 in) circles on baking parchment; place on 2 baking sheets. In a large bowl, whisk egg whites until stiff.

Whisk in half the sugar and then gently fold in rest of the sugar, vanilla essence, vinegar and cornflour with a metal spoon. Spread or pipe meringue over circles on parchment on baking sheets. Bake in oven for 1-1½ hours or until dry. Transfer to a wire rack to cool. Meanwhile, prepare filling. In a bowl, whisk cream until thick. Peel kiwi fruit and slice. Halve strawberries. In a separate bowl, mix fruit together gently. To assemble gâteau, place one meringue circle, flat side down, on a serving plate.

Spread it with most of the cream, reserving a little for piping. Place most of the fruit on top of the cream, reserving some pieces for decoration. Top with second meringue circle, flat side down. Pipe remaining cream decoratively on top of the gâteau and decorate with remaining pieces of fruit. Serve immediately.

Serves 8.

Total Cals/Kj: 1615/6785   Total fat: 73.0 g
Cals/Kj per portion: 202/848   Fat per portion: 9.1 g

— STRAWBERRY PROFITEROLES —

70 g (2½ oz/½ cup) plain flour
55 g (2 oz/¼ cup) low fat spread
2 eggs, beaten
150 ml (5 fl oz/⅔ cup) reduced fat double
   (heavy) cream
225 g (8 oz) strawberries
25 g (1 oz/ 2 tablespoons) icing sugar

Preheat oven to 200C (400F/Gas 6). Line 2 baking sheets with baking parchment. Sift flour onto a plate. Put low fat spread and 150 ml (5 fl oz/⅔ cup) water into a saucepan, heat gently until fat has melted, then bring to the boil. Remove from heat, add flour and beat until mixture leaves the sides of the pan.

Gradually beat in eggs until mixture is smooth and shiny. Put mixture into a piping bag fitted with a medium plain nozzle and pipe walnut-sized balls onto prepared baking sheets. Bake in oven for 20-25 minutes until brown and crisp. Make a slit in side of each profiterole to allow steam to escape, then cool on a wire rack. In a bowl, whisk cream until stiff and spoon into a piping bag fitted with a medium plain nozzle. Pipe some cream into each profiterole.

Halve strawberries and place some strawberries into each profiterole. Pile profiteroles into a pyramid on a serving plate and dust with sifted icing sugar. Serve immediately.

Serves 8.

Total Cals/Kj: 962/5494   Total fat: 75.5 g
Cals/Kj per portion: 120/687   Fat per portion: 9.4 g

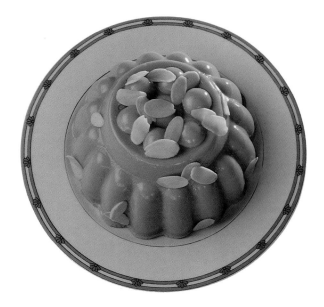

COFFEE ALMOND BLANCMANGE

12 teaspoons cornflour
55 g (2 oz/¼ cup) caster sugar
550 ml (20 fl oz/2½ cups) skimmed milk
2 teaspoons instant coffee powder
15 g (½ oz/3 teaspoons) low fat spread
25 g (1 oz/¼ cup) flaked almonds, toasted

In a bowl, blend cornflour and sugar with 2 tablespoons milk. Place remaining milk in a saucepan and heat until almost boiling.

Pour the hot milk onto cornflour mixture, stirring well. Return mixture to saucepan and heat gently until mixture boils and thickens, stirring continuously. In a small bowl, blend coffee powder with 1 tablespoon warm water. Add to custard with low fat spread and cook for a further 3 minutes.

Pour mixture into a 850 ml (30 fl oz/3¾ cup) wetted mould and leave to cool. Chill in the refrigerator until set. To serve, turn out mould onto a serving plate and sprinkle with flaked almonds.

Serves 4.

Total Cals/Kj: 823/3473   Total fat: 20.8 g
Cals/Kj per portion: 206/868   Fat per portion: 5.2 g

– BANANA & PINEAPPLE TRIFLE –

6 teaspoons reduced sugar peach or apricot jam
6 trifle sponge cakes
225 g (8 oz) can pineapple cubes in fruit juice
2 tablespoons brandy
2 bananas
12.5 g (½ oz) packet sugar-free jelly crystals
300 ml (10 fl oz/1¼ cups) low fat ready-made
  cold custard
300 ml (10 fl oz/1¼ cups) very low fat fromage frais
crystallized pineapple and angelica, to decorate

Spread jam on trifle sponge cakes and cut into
fingers. Place in base of a glass serving dish.
Drain pineapple cubes, reserving juice.

Mix together pineapple juice and brandy and
pour over sponge cakes. Peel and slice
bananas. Arrange pineapple cubes and
banana slices over sponge cakes. Dissolve
jelly crystals in 300 ml (10 fl oz/1¼ cups)
boiling water, then make up liquid to 550 ml
(20 fl oz/2½ cups) with cold water.

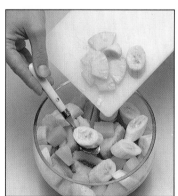

Cool and then pour over fruit. Chill in the
refrigerator until set. In a bowl, mix together
cold custard and fromage frais. Spread over
jelly, decorate with crystallized pineapple
and angelica and serve.

Serves 6.

Total Cals/Kj: 1365/5543　　　Total fat: 8.5 g
Cals/Kj per portion: 228/924　　Fat per portion: 1.4 g

Note: Stale leftover sponge cake can be used
instead of trifle sponge cakes.

TROPICAL MELON CUPS

1 large galia or ogen melon
225 g (8 oz) pineapple
1 papaya
10 fresh dates
2 kiwi fruit
300 ml (10 fl oz/1 ¼ cups) unsweetened tropical
    fruit juice
300 ml (10 fl oz/1 ¼ cups) dry sherry

Cut melon in half crosswise in a zig-zag pattern and remove seeds. Hollow out flesh using a melon baller and place in a large bowl.

Prepare remaining fruit. Skin and core pineapple and chop into small cubes. Peel, seed and chop papaya roughly. Halve and stone dates and peel and slice kiwi fruit. Mix fruit with melon flesh. Pile fruit into melon halves, serving any leftover fruit separately.

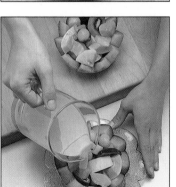

In a measuring jug, mix together fruit juice and sherry and pour over fruit. Chill in the refrigerator until ready to serve.

Serves 6.

Total Cals/Kj: 1137/4775   Total fat: 2.8 g
Cals/Kj per portion: 189/796   Fat per portion: 0.4 g

──BLACKCURRANT MOUSSE──

225 g (8 oz) blackcurrants
450 ml (16 fl oz/2 cups) skimmed milk
85 g (3 oz/⅓ cup) caster sugar
3 teaspoons cornflour
pinch of salt
3 egg yolks
5 teaspoons powdered gelatine
300 ml (10 fl oz/1 ¼ cups) reduced fat single
    (light) cream
mint leaves and currants, to decorate

Place blackcurrants in a saucepan with 2
tablespoons water and cook gently until just
soft. Cool, then purée in a blender or food
processor until smooth.

In another saucepan, blend together milk,
sugar, cornflour, salt and egg yolks. Heat
mixture gently, stirring continuously, until it
thickens. Bring to the boil and boil for 1
minute. Sprinkle gelatine over 3 tablespoons
water in a small bowl and leave for 2-3
minutes to soften. Stand bowl in a saucepan
of hot water and stir until the gelatine has
dissolved. Cool slightly. Add gelatine and
blackcurrant purée to custard mixture.

In a bowl, mix custard mixture and cream
together lightly. Pour mixture into a wetted
1.2 litre (40 fl oz/5 cup) mould and chill in
the refrigerator until set. To serve, turn out
onto a plate and decorate with mint leaves
and currants.

Serves 6.

Total Cals/Kj: 1254/5276   Total fat: 47.3 g
Cals/Kj per portion: 209/879   Fat per portion: 7.9 g

CAROB HAZELNUT CHEESECAKE

85 g (3 oz/³⁄₄ cup) wholemeal plain flour
25 g (1 oz/¹⁄₄ cup) carob flour
55 g (2 oz/¹⁄₄ cup) low fat spread
115 g (4 oz) plain (dark) carob drops
225 g (8 oz) low fat soft cheese
150 ml (5 fl oz/²⁄₃ cup) very low fat fromage frais
12 teaspoons thick honey
25 g (1 oz/¹⁄₄ cup) hazelnuts, chopped
2 eggs, separated
1 tablespoon icing sugar

Preheat oven to 180C (350F/Gas 4). Sift both flours into a bowl. Rub in low fat spread until mixture resembles breadcrumbs. Add enough water to make a soft dough.

On a lightly floured surface, roll out pastry and use to line base of a 20 cm (8 in) loose-bottomed flan tin. Melt carob drops in a small bowl set over a saucepan of simmering water. Allow to cool. In a large bowl, mix together melted carob, soft cheese, fromage frais, honey, nuts and egg yolks until well combined. In another bowl, whisk egg whites until stiff and fold gently into carob mixture, using a metal spoon.

Pour mixture over pastry base. Bake in oven for 45 minutes until firm to touch. Transfer to a wire rack to cool, then chill in the refrigerator. To serve, remove cheesecake from tin and dust with sifted icing sugar.

Serves 8.

Total Cals/Kj: 1753/7337   Total fat: 74.2 g
Cals/Kj per portion: 219/917   Fat per portion: 9.2 g

Note: Serve with yogurt and chopped nuts, if wished, but it will add extra calories.

— TROPICAL FRUIT CLUSTERS —

1 mango
1 orange
1 banana
1 cooking apple
55 g (2 oz/⅓ cup) soft brown sugar
8 sheets filo pastry
55 g (2 oz/¼ cup) low fat spread, melted
1 tablespoon icing sugar

Preheat oven to 200C (400F/Gas 6). Prepare filling. Peel, stone and chop mango and put in a bowl. Segment orange, squeezing out any juice and add to mango. Peel and slice banana. Peel core and grate apple.

Add to mango mixture with sugar and mix well. Set aside. To make each fruit cluster, cut each filo sheet in half crosswise to make two 10 cm (4 in) squares (total of 16 squares). Brush 2 squares of pastry lightly with melted fat and place one on top of the other diagonally. Place some filling in centre of the pastry.

Gather up pastry over filling and tie with string. Place cluster on a greased baking sheet and brush lightly with melted fat. Repeat with remaining pastry squares and filling to make 8 clusters. Bake in oven for 30 minutes until golden brown and crisp. Carefully remove string from each cluster before serving. Dust with sifted icing sugar just before serving. Serve hot or cold.

Makes 8.

Cals/Kj per cluster: 162/681   Fat per cluster: 3.4 g

— WHITE WINE & GRAPE JELLY —

5 teaspoons powdered gelatine
55 g (2 oz/¼ cup) caster sugar
300 ml (10 fl oz/1¼ cups) unsweetened apple juice
300 ml (10 fl oz/1¼ cups) medium dry white wine
300 g (10 oz) green seedless grapes, skinned and halved
mint sprigs and small bunches red seedless grapes,
   to decorate

Sprinkle gelatine over 3 tablespoons water in a small bowl and leave for 2-3 minutes to soften. Stand bowl in a saucepan of hot water and stir until gelatine has dissolved. Cool slightly.

Place sugar in a saucepan with apple juice. Heat gently until sugar has dissolved. Add wine and gelatine to apple juice and mix well. Set aside until just beginning to set. Stir grapes into the jelly mixture and pour into 4 wetted 300 ml (10 fl oz/1¼ cup) moulds. Chill in the refrigerator until set.

To serve, turn moulds out onto serving plates and decorate with mint sprigs and small bunches of red grapes. Serve with low fat fromage frais or Greek yogurt, if wished.

Serves 4.

Total Cals/Kj: 812/3439   Total fat: 0.6 g
Cals/Kj per portion: 203/860   Fat per portion: 0.1 g

Note: Stand jellied desserts at room temperature for 30 minutes before serving, to take off the chill and restore the flavour.

──────FRESH FRUIT PLATTER──────

20 g (³/₄ oz/4 teaspoons) low fat spread
6 teaspoons plain flour
300 ml (10 fl oz/1¼ cups) semi-skimmed milk
25 g (1 oz/5 teaspoons) caster sugar
1 mango, peeled, stoned and puréed
1 melon
4 kiwi fruit
2 peaches
4 red dessert plums
2 bananas
115 g (4 oz) raspberries
175 g (6 oz) strawberries
225 g (8 oz) green grapes, in small bunches

To make mango sauce, melt fat gently in a saucepan. Remove from heat, stir in flour, then gradually stir in milk, blending well. Bring slowly to the boil, stirring continuously, until mixture thickens. Simmer for 3 minutes. Remove from heat and add sugar and mango purée, mixing well. Serve mango sauce hot or cold with fruit. To prepare fruit, peel melon, remove seeds and cut into small slices. Peel kiwi fruit and quarter each fruit.

Peel and stone peaches, then cut each into 8 pieces. Stone and quarter plums. Peel bananas and cut into long thin slices. Arrange selection of fruit decoratively on a large platter or serving dish. Serve immediately with hot or cold mango sauce.

Serves 8.

Total Cals/Kj: 1438/6590   Total fat: 13.4 g
Cals/Kj per portion: 180/824   Fat per portion: 1.7 g

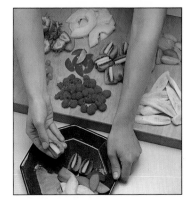

LEMON CHEESE FLAN

150 g (5 oz) semi-sweet wheatmeal biscuits
45 g (1½ oz/1½ tablespoons) low fat spread, melted
3 teaspoons powdered gelatine
150 ml (5 fl oz/⅔ cup) reduced fat double
   (heavy) cream
300 ml (10 fl oz/1¼ cups) very low fat fromage frais
115 g (4 oz/½ cup) skimmed milk soft cheese
55 g (2 oz/¼ cup) caster sugar
grated rind and juice of 2 lemons
lemon slices and mint sprigs, to decorate

In a bowl, crush biscuits to crumbs and mix with melted low fat spread. Press mixture over base of a 20 cm (8 in) loose-bottomed flan tin. Chill in the refrigerator.

Sprinkle gelatine over 3 tablespoons water in a small bowl and leave for 2-3 minutes to soften. Stand bowl in a saucepan of hot water and stir until gelatine has dissolved. Cool slightly. Place cream, fromage frais, soft cheese, sugar, lemon rind and juice and gelatine into a blender or food processor and blend until smooth and well mixed.

Pour over biscuit base, level surface and chill in the refrigerator until set. To serve, remove carefully from tin and place on a serving plate. Decorate with lemon slices and mint sprigs before serving.

Serves 8.

Total Cals/Kj: 1777/7444   Total fat: 86.0 g
Cals/Kj per portion: 222/931   Fat per portion: 10.7 g

— ORIENTAL FRUIT PAVLOVA —

3 egg whites
175 g (6 oz/¾ cup) caster sugar
few drops vanilla essence
½ teaspoon white wine vinegar
1 teaspoon cornflour
300 ml (10 fl oz/1¼ cups) reduced fat double (heavy) cream
350 g (12 oz) prepared fresh fruit, such as carambola (starfruit), lychees, mango, melon and dates

Preheat oven to 150C (300F/Gas 2). Draw a 17.5 cm (7 in) circle on a sheet of non-stick baking parchment and place paper, mark-side down, on a baking sheet. In a large bowl, whisk egg whites until stiff.

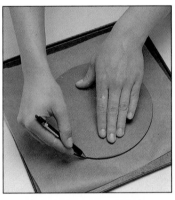

Whisk in half the sugar then, using a metal spoon, gently fold in remaining sugar together with vanilla essence, vinegar and cornflour. Spread meringue over the circle on the paper, building sides up higher than the centre. Bake in oven for 1-1½ hours until meringue is crisp and dry. Cool on a wire rack, then carefully peel off the paper.

In a bowl, whip cream until stiff. Place meringue on a serving plate, pile cream into the centre and arrange prepared fresh fruit decoratively on top. Serve immediately.

Serves 8.

Total Cals/Kj: 1713/7208   Total fat: 72.4 g
Cals/Kj per portion: 214/901   Fat per portion: 9.0 g

Note: An electric or hand whisk can be used to make meringue mixtures.

CHOC & STRAWBERRY ROULADE

3 eggs
115 g (4 oz/½ cup) caster sugar
85 g (3 oz/¾ cup) plain flour
25 g (1 oz/¼ cup) cocoa powder
225 g (8 oz/1 cup) skimmed milk soft cheese
12 teaspoons reduced sugar strawberry jam
175 g (6 oz) strawberries
1 tablespoon icing sugar

Preheat oven to 200C (400F/Gas 6). Grease a
32.5 × 22.5 cm (13 × 9 in) Swiss roll tin.
Line with greaseproof paper and grease the
paper. In a bowl placed over a pan of hot
water, whisk eggs and sugar until creamy.

Remove bowl from heat and whisk until cool.
Sift flour and cocoa powder over egg mixture,
add 1 tablespoon hot water and fold in gently
with a metal spoon. Pour mixture into prepared tin and tilt tin to level the surface. Bake
in oven for 12-15 minutes until well risen,
golden brown and firm to touch. Turn out
onto a sheet of greaseproof paper, cut off crisp
edges and roll up with paper inside. Leave to
cool.

Unroll gently and spread with soft cheese and
jam. Slice strawberries and place on jam,
reserving a few for decoration. Roll up again
and place on a serving dish. Dust with sifted
icing sugar and decorate with remaining
strawberry slices before serving.

Serves 6.

Total Cals/Kj: 1501/6336   Total fat: 30.8 g
Cals/Kj per portion: 250/1056   Fat per portion: 5.1 g

—MELON WITH GINGER SAUCE—

1 small charentais or honeydew melon
25 g (1 oz) crystallized ginger
150 ml (5 fl oz/²⁄₃ cup) ginger wine
55 g (2 oz/¹⁄₂ cup) hazelnuts, chopped

Cut melon in half, remove seeds and scoop flesh from melon, using a melon baller. Place melon balls in a bowl.

Chop crystallized ginger finely and add to melon balls, with ginger wine. Mix gently, but well. Chill in the refrigerator for at least 2 hours, stirring occasionally.

Spoon melon and juice into 4 glass serving dishes and sprinkle with chopped hazelnuts to serve.

Serves 4.

Total Cals/Kj: 903/3744   Total fat: 36.7 g
Cals/Kj per portion: 226/936   Fat per portion: 9.1 g

Note: Nuts can be chopped more easily if they are fresh, warm and moist.

—APPLE & ALMOND STRUDEL—

700 g (1½ lb) cooking apples
1 tablespoon lemon juice
85 g (3 oz/½ cup) raisins
55 g (2 oz/⅓ cup) soft brown sugar
2 teaspoons ground mixed spice
8 sheets filo pastry
55 g (2 oz/¼ cup) low fat spread, melted
115 g (4 oz/2 cups) fresh breadcrumbs
25 g (1 oz/¼ cup) flaked almonds
25 g (1 oz/6 teaspoons) icing sugar

Preheat oven to 190C (375F/Gas 5). Peel, core and slice apples. Place in a bowl and sprinkle with lemon juice. Add raisins, sugar and mixed spice and mix well.

Place one sheet of pastry on a sheet of non-stick baking parchment and brush lightly with melted fat. Place another sheet on top and layer all 8 sheets of pastry on top of one another, brushing each one lightly with melted fat. Sprinkle breadcrumbs over pastry, leaving a 2.5 cm (1 in) border uncovered all around edge. Spread apple mixture over breadcrumbs, then fold border edges over fruit mixture. With a long side towards you, using the non-stick paper, roll up strudel.

Carefully place it on a greased baking sheet, seam-side down, shaping the roll into a horseshoe, if wished. Brush roll lightly with melted fat and sprinkle with flaked almonds. Bake in oven for about 40 minutes until golden brown. Dust with sifted icing sugar to serve. Serve hot or cold with reduced fat cream.

Serves 8.

Total Cals/Kj: 1974/8822   Total fat: 43.9 g
Cals/Kj per portion: 247/1103   Fat per portion: 5.4 g

– GLAZED BLUEBERRY TARTLETS –

150 g (5 oz) semi-sweet wheatmeal biscuits
25 g (1 oz/¼ cup) ground almonds
55 g (2 oz/⅓ cup) soft brown sugar
55 g (2 oz/¼ cup) low fat spread, melted
350 g (12 oz) blueberries
9 tablespoons redcurrant jelly
1 tablespoon icing sugar (optional)
mint leaves, to decorate

In a bowl, crush biscuits to crumbs and mix together with almonds, sugar and melted low fat spread.

Press mixture into 12 greased deep patty tins and chill in the refrigerator until firm. Carefully remove tartlet cases from tins and pile blueberries into the cases.

In a saucepan, warm redcurrant jelly with 2 tablespoons water. Brush over blueberries to glaze. Serve blueberry tartlets dusted with sifted icing sugar, if wished. Decorate with mint leaves.

Makes 12.

Cals/Kj per tartlet: 126/528   Fat per tartlet: 5.7 g

—SPICY SULTANA CHEESECAKE—

70 g (2½ oz) low fat spread
55 g (2 oz/⅓ cup) soft brown sugar
130 g (4½ oz/1⅓ cups) rolled oats
225 g (8 oz/1 cup) skimmed milk soft cheese
3 eggs, separated
1 teaspoon ground mixed spice
25 g (1 oz/¼ cup) plain flour, sifted
150 ml (5 fl oz/⅔ cup) reduced fat double
   (heavy) cream
grated rind and juice of 1 lemon
85 g (3 oz/⅓ cup) caster sugar
85 g (3 oz/½ cup) sultanas
1 tablespoon icing sugar

In a saucepan, melt low fat spread and soft brown sugar together over a low heat.

Remove from heat and add oats. Mix well. Press mixture over base of a 20 cm (8 in) loose-bottomed tin. Chill in the refrigerator until it is firm. Preheat oven to 160C (325F/Gas 3). Place soft cheese, egg yolks, mixed spice, flour, cream, lemon rind and juice and caster sugar into a blender or food processor. Blend until smooth and well mixed. Transfer mixture to a bowl and stir in sultanas.

In a separate bowl, whisk egg whites until stiff and fold gently into cheese mixture, using a metal spoon. Pour over base and level surface. Bake in oven for 1-1½ hours until golden brown and firm to touch. Allow to cool, then remove from tin. Place on a serving plate and chill until ready to serve. Serve dusted with sifted icing sugar.

Serves 10.

Total Cals/Kj: 2555/10711   Total fat: 98.8 g
Cals/Kj per portion: 255/1071   Fat per portion: 9.8 g

—— VINE FRUITS GÂTEAU ——

4 eggs
115 g (4 oz/½ cup) caster sugar
115 g (4 oz/1 cup) plain flour
225 ml (8 fl oz/1 cup) reduced fat double
    (heavy) cream
115 g (4 oz) black grapes
½ small cantaloupe melon
2 kiwi fruit
1 tablespoon icing sugar

Preheat oven to 190C (375F/Gas 5). Grease a
20 cm (8 in) deep cake tin. Place eggs and
sugar in a large bowl and whisk until thick,
pale and creamy. Sift flour over mixture and
fold in gently, using a metal spoon.

Pour mixture into prepared tin, tilting tin to
level surface. Bake in oven for 25-30 minutes
until well risen and firm to touch. Turn out
and cool on a wire rack. In a bowl, whisk
cream until stiff. To prepare fruit, halve and
seed grapes. Peel, seed and dice melon, and
peel and slice kiwi fruit. In a bowl, gently mix
fruit together. To assemble gâteau, cut the
sponge cake across into 3 layers. Place one
slice on a serving plate, cut-side up. Spread
one third of the cream over base, then
arrange some fruit on top.

Place a sponge cake on top and spread this
with another third of cream. Arrange fruit on
top. Place remaining sponge cake slice on
top, cut-side down. Spread or pipe remaining
cream over top and arrange remaining fruit
decoratively over cream. Dust fruit with
sifted icing sugar and serve immediately.

Serves 10.

Total Cals/Kj: 2147/8995   Total fat: 89.4 g
Cals/Kj per portion: 215/899   Fat per portion: 8.9 g

INDEX